Richard Clarke is a barrister at Landmark Chambers who specialises in all aspects of property litigation including commercial and residential landlord and tenant, easements, covenants, boundaries and injunctions.

A Practical Guide to Alienation, Alteration and User Covenants in Commercial Property

A Practical Guide to Alienation, Alteration and User Covenants in Commercial Property

Richard Clarke
Barrister, Middle Temple
LLB (Hons) BCL (Oxon)

Law Brief Publishing

Published 2023 by Law Brief Publishing, an imprint of Law Brief Publishing Ltd
30 The Parks
Minehead
Somerset
TA24 8BT

www.lawbriefpublishing.com

Paperback: 978-1-914608-77-3

For Joshua

PREFACE

Three of the most important issues in any landlord and tenant relationship are (1) how the property let may be used; (2) whether and how the property may be altered by the tenant; and (3) how the tenant may deal with its interest in the property, such as whether the tenant may transfer its interest to somebody else or sublet. A well drafted commercial lease will make express provision for each of these matters. However, not all leases do. Further, even when leases do, issues around alienation, alteration and user remain a frequent cause of dispute between landlords and tenants. The importance of these matters to tenants has also been acknowledged by Parliament, which has intervened by statute in the regulation of these areas.

The aim of this book is to provide an efficient, practical guide to workings of alienation, alteration and user covenants in commercial property. Each chapter has been written so that the busy reader can quickly extract the key points that they need regarding the law and the issues that can arise. Each chapter also ends with a summary of the essential points.

I have endeavoured to state the law as it stands, for England and Wales, on 01/02/2023.

Richard Clarke
April 2023

CONTENTS

CHAPTER ONE

THE INTERPRETATION OF LEASES

1. Legal disputes are often won or lost on the true meaning of a few sentences of text. It is therefore not surprising that the principles which govern the interpretation of legal documents have been considered by the courts at length over the centuries. Helpfully, it is not necessary to trace this lengthy history as in a series of recent cases the Supreme Court has authoritatively restated the applicable principles.

<u>The modern approach to interpreting leases</u>

2. In his well-known speech in *Investors Compensation Scheme Ltd v West Bromwich Building Society*[1], Lord Hoffman noted that recent cases[2] had brought about a *"fundamental change"* in the courts' approach to interpreting legal documents: old technicalities had been discarded and, subject to one exception, documents should be interpreted by judges using the same *"common sense principles by which any serious utterance would be interpreted in ordinary life."* Lord Hoffman summarised the principles[3] as being that:

   "(1) Interpretation is the ascertainment of the meaning which the document would convey to a reasonable person having all the background

---

1 [1998] 1 W.L.R. 896; [1998] 1 All ER 98.

2 Particularly the speeches of Lord Wilberforce in *Prenn v. Simmonds* [1971] 1 WLR 1381 at 1384–1386 and *Reardon Smith Line Ltd. v. Yngvar Hansen-Tangen* [1976] 1 WLR 989.

3 At 912-913.

knowledge which would reasonably have been available to the parties in the situation in which they were at the time of the contract.

(2) The background was famously referred to by Lord Wilberforce as the "matrix of fact," but this phrase is, if anything, an understated description of what the background may include. Subject to the requirement that it should have been reasonably available to the parties and to the exception to be mentioned next, it includes absolutely anything which would have affected the way in which the language of the document would have been understood by a reasonable man.

(3) The law excludes from the admissible background the previous negotiations of the parties and their declarations of subjective intent. They are admissible only in an action for rectification. The law makes this distinction for reasons of practical policy and, in this respect only, legal interpretation differs from the way we would interpret utterances in ordinary life. The boundaries of this exception are in some respects unclear. But this is not the occasion on which to explore them.

(4) The meaning which a document (or any other utterance) would convey to a reasonable man is not the same thing as the meaning of its words. The meaning of words is a matter of dictionaries and grammars; the meaning of the document is what the parties using those words against the relevant background would reasonably have been understood to mean. The background may not merely enable the reasonable man to choose between the possible meanings of words which are ambiguous but even (as occasionally happens in ordinary life) to conclude that the parties must, for whatever reason, have used the wrong words or syntax: see Mannai Investments Co. Ltd. V. Eagle Star Life Assurance Co. Ltd. [1997] A.C. 749.

(5) The "rule" that words should be given their "natural and ordinary meaning" reflects the common sense proposition that we do not easily accept that people have made linguistic mistakes, particularly in formal documents. On the other hand, if one would nevertheless conclude from the background that something must have gone wrong with the language,

the law does not require judges to attribute to the parties an intention which they plainly could not have had..."

3. The Supreme Court returned to this issue in *Rainy Sky SA v Kookmin Bank*[4]. Lord Clarke, giving the unanimous judgment of the court, referred back to the *Investors Compensation Scheme* summary[5] and agreed that:

   a) *"The ultimate aim of interpreting a provision in a contract, especially a commercial contract, is to determine what the parties meant by the language used, which involves ascertaining what a reasonable person would have understood the parties to have meant"*;

   b) The relevant reasonable person is one who has all the background knowledge which would reasonably have been available to the parties in the situation in which they were at the time of the contract[6].

4. The issue for the Supreme Court in *Rainy Sky* was the role of business common sense when interpreting a commercial agreement. Lord Clarke, reviewing the authorities[7], held the true principle to be that:

"The language used by the parties will often have more than one potential meaning. I would accept the submission made on behalf of the appellants that the exercise of construction is essentially one unitary exercise in which the court must consider the language used and ascertain what a reasonable person, that is a person who has all the background knowledge which would reasonably have been available to the parties in the

---

4 [2011] UKSC 50; [2011] 1 WLR 2900; [2012] 1 All ER 1137.

5 As well as to similar statements in *Chartbrook Ltd v Persimmon Homes Ltd* [2009] AC 1101 paragraphs 21—26; *Mannai Investment Co Ltd v Eagle Star Life Assurance Co Ltd* [1997] AC 749 and *Pink Floyd Music Ltd v EMI Records Ltd* [2010] EWCA Civ 1429 paragraph 17.

6 Paragraph 14.

7 Paragraphs 15-30.

situation in which they were at the time of the contract, would have understood the parties to have meant. In doing so, the court must have regard to all the relevant surrounding circumstances. If there are two possible constructions, the court is entitled to prefer the construction which is consistent with business common sense and to reject the other."[8]

5. Lord Clarke further explained that:

    a) Where the parties have used unambiguous language, the court must apply it, whether or not the result accords with commercial sense or amounts to a bad bargain for one of the parties[9];

    b) However, the more improbable the result, the clearer the language required before the court will find that is the meaning the parties intended[10]. In others words, the court will strive to attribute clauses with a meaning which accords with business common sense;

    c) Correspondingly, the poorer the drafting, the less willing the court will be to be driven by semantic niceties to attribute to the parties an improbable and unbusinesslike intention.[11]

6. In *Arnold v Britton*[12], the Supreme Court returned to the principles of interpretation in the context of leases specifically. As in the cases discussed above, Lord Neuberger recognised the role of the court as being to identify the intention of the parties by reference to *"what a reasonable person having all the background knowledge which would have been available to the parties would have understood them to be using*

---

8 Paragraph 21. See too paragraph 30.

9 See paragraphs 19 – 20 and 23.

10 See paragraphs 24-25.

11 Paragraph 26.

12 [2015] UKSC 36; [2015] AC 1619; [2015] 2 WLR 1593; [2016] 1 All ER 1.

the language in the contract to mean", assessed in light of: (i) the natural and ordinary meaning of the clause; (ii) any other relevant provisions of the lease; (iii) the overall purpose of the clause and the lease; (iv) the facts and circumstances known or assumed by the parties at the time the document was executed and (v) commercial common sense, but disregarding any subjective evidence of any party's intentions[13].

7. At paragraphs 16-23, Lord Neuberger emphasised seven factors relevant to the interpretative exercise:

    a) Commercial common sense and surrounding circumstances "*should not be invoked to undervalue the importance of the language of the provision which is to be construed*"[14]. Interpreting a provision involves identifying what the parties meant through the eyes of a reasonable reader, and save in an unusual case, that meaning is "*most obviously to be gleaned from the language of the provision*". Unlike commercial common sense and the surrounding circumstances, the parties have direct control over the language they use in a contract;

    b) The less the clear the words used, the more willing the court will be to depart from their natural meaning. The clearer the natural meaning, the more difficult it will be to justify departing from it. Courts should not, however, search for "*drafting infelicities in order to facilitate a departure from the natural meaning*"[15];

    c) Commercial common sense should not be invoked retrospectively: "*The mere fact that a contractual arrangement, if interpreted according to its natural language, has worked out*

[13] Paragraph 15.

[14] Paragraph 17.

[15] Paragraph 18.

badly, or even disastrously, for one of the parties is not a reason for departing from the natural language. Commercial common sense is only relevant to the extent of how matters would or could have been perceived by the parties, or by reasonable people in the position of the parties, as at the date that the contract was made."[16]

d) Whilst commercial common sense is a very important factor for the court to take into account when interpreting a contract, a court should be *"very slow"* to reject the natural meaning of a provision *"simply because it appears to be a very imprudent term for one of the parties to have agreed, even ignoring the benefit of wisdom of hindsight"*. The purpose of the court is to identify what the parties have agreed, not what the court thinks they should have agreed[17];

e) When interpreting a contract, the court may only take into account facts or circumstances which existed at the time the contract was made and which were known or reasonably available to both parties[18];

f) Where an event occurs which was not intended or contemplated by the parties, if it is clear what the parties would have intended, the court will give effect to that intention[19];

g) There is no special rule of interpretation that service charge clauses should be interpreted restrictively[20].

---

[16] Paragraph 19.

[17] Paragraph 20.

[18] Paragraph 21.

[19] Paragraph 22.

[20] Paragraph 23.

8. In *Wood v Capita Insurance Services Ltd*[21], the Supreme Court again confirmed the above principles[22], which it declined to reformulate[23], and confirmed that there is no difference between the approaches set out in *Rainy Sky* and *Arnold*: they were saying the same thing.[24]

<u>The interpretation of leases protected by registration</u>

9. When a lease is granted out of a registered title for a term of more than seven years, the disposition must be completed by registration.[25] Where a new lease is granted for a term of more than seven years out of an unregistered freehold or leasehold estate for valuable or other consideration, by way of gift, or pursuant to an order of any court, it must likewise be completed by registration.[26]

10. Where a lease is registered at HM Land Registry, special considerations apply to its interpretation. As already explained, when interpreting a lease, the court will ask what meaning it would convey to a reasonable person having all the background knowledge available to both parties at the date of the lease, but excluding the content of previous negotiations. Where a lease is protected by registration, in addition to excluding the content of prior negotiations from the admissible background, the court should give no weight to extrinsic documents or circumstances which were not publicly accessible, even where the dispute is between the original parties to the lease.

11. This restriction originates from the decision of the Court of Appeal in *Cherry Tree Investments Ltd v Landmain Ltd*[27]. In that case, by a

---

[21] [2017] UKSC 24; [2017] AC 1173; [2017] 2 WLR 1095; [2017] 4 All ER 615.

[22] See *Wood* paragraphs 10.

[23] *Wood* paragraph 9.

[24] *Wood* paragraph 14.

[25] Land Registration Act 2002 s27(2)(b).

[26] Land Registration Act 2002 s4(1)(c).

[27] [2012] EWCA Civ 736; [2013] Ch 305; [2013] 2 WLR 481.

facility agreement a lender granted a bridging loan to the defendant (Landmain Ltd), the registered proprietor of a property. The facility agreement provided that the defendant's obligations should be secured by a legal charge over the defendant's property, and varied the statutory power of sale implied into the charge by s101 of the Law of Property Act 1925. A legal charge was executed the same day which made no reference to the facility agreement. The legal charge was registered at HM Land Registry, but the facility agreement was not. The lender subsequently sold the property to Cherry Tree in reliance on the power of sale in the registered charge, read together with the modifications in the facility agreement. The validity of the sale relied upon the facility agreement having varied or extended the statutory power of sale in the legal charge. The Court of Appeal held that the court at first instance had been wrong to treat the registered charge as including the extended power of sale. Weight could not be given to the facility agreement when interpreting the registered charge.

12. Lewison LJ began by recognising that the true meaning of the charge could not depend upon whether the parties to the dispute were the original contracting parties or successors to the original parties/third parties:

"The question, then, is what does the registered charge mean? Whatever it means, it has always meant what it means. A contract cannot mean one thing when it is made and another thing following court proceedings. Nor, in my judgment, can it mean one thing to some people (e g the parties to it) and another thing to others who might be affected by it."[28]

13. Lewison LJ held the facility agreement to be admissible evidence and proceeded to address what weight the court should give to it. Concluding that no weight should be given to it, the context of the charge being protected by registration was held to be crucial. This was because:

---

[28] Paragraph 99.

"...The reasonable reader's background knowledge would, of course, include the knowledge that the charge would be registered in a publicly accessible register upon which third parties might be expected to rely. In other words a publicly registered document is addressed to anyone who wishes to inspect it. His knowledge would include the knowledge that in so far as documents or copy documents were retained by the registrar they were to be taken as containing all material terms, and that a person inspecting the register could not call for originals. The reasonable reader would also understand that the parties had a choice about what they put into the public domain and what they kept private. He would conclude that matters which the parties chose to keep private should not influence the parts of the bargain that they chose to make public... a third party contemplating dealing with the land has no access to collateral documents.[29]

14. The *Cherry Tree* principle has been subsequently applied to the interpretation of leases by the High Court in *Murphy v LB of Lambeth*[30]. In *Murphy*, the court considered the extent of the property demised by a lease. The lease had been granted to the claimant's predecessor in title pursuant to the right to buy, and a dispute arose between the successor in title and the local authority freeholder over whether the demise included a basement. One of the issues before the court was whether a notice served pursuant to s125 of Housing Act 1985 ("s125 notice") as part of the right to buy process and which described the property subject to the right to buy should be given weight when interpreting the lease. The s125 notice made no mention of the basement, whereas the recitals to the lease did. The local authority sought to rely on the s125 notice, particularly where the lease was expressly stated to be made under the Housing Act 1985.

---

29 Paragraph 130.

30 [2016] EWHC 780 (Ch).

15. Applying *Cherry Tree*, the court held that no weight should be given the s125 notice: the lease was subject to registration and any purchaser of the lease would not be entitled to see a s125 notice.[31]

<u>The interpretation of leases where there are mistakes in the drafting</u>

16. Mistakes in the drafting of legal documents can be corrected by means of an action for rectification, the workings of which are outside the scope of this book. However, in limited cases an obvious drafting mistake can be corrected through interpretation, rather than by an action for rectification.

17. For a drafting mistake to be corrected by interpretation, there must be a clear mistake on the face of the document and it must be clear what correction ought to be made to cure the mistake.[32] These requirements were confirmed by Lord Hoffmann in *Chartbrook v. Persimmon Homes Ltd*[33], who explained that the ability to correct mistakes by construction is part and parcel of the process of interpreting a document, not a separate branch of the law or a summary version of an action for rectification[34]. It follows that, in deciding whether there has been a clear mistake, regard may be had to the admissible background and context - the court is not confined to the text of the instrument itself[35].

18. The ability to correct the literal meaning of a provision where it is clear both that a mistake has been made and what the provision was

---

31 See paragraphs 28 to 32.

32 See the judgment of Brightman LJ in *East v Pantiles (Plant Hire) Ltd* [1982] 2 EGLR 111. See too *Chartbrook v. Persimmon Homes Ltd* [2009] UKHL 38 at paragraphs 22-23.

33 [2009] UKHL 38; [2009] 1 AC 1101; [2009] 3 WLR 267; [2009] 4 All ER 677.

34 Paragraph 23.

35 Paragraph 24.

intended to say is now sometimes referred to as the 'Chartbrook principle'[36].

19. Two important restrictions to the Chartbrook principle should be kept in mind:

    a) That a lease provision lacks commercial commonsense is not by itself enough to show that there has been a clear error in the language used. Nor is it sufficient that it was imprudent for one of the parties to agree to the term as drafted.[37] For a clear mistake to be shown, the literal meaning of the language used should produce a result which is irrational, arbitrary, nonsensical or absurd[38];

    b) Even if it is clear that a mistake has been made, the court will not correct the mistake by construction if it is not clear what the parties in fact intended. In such a case, the literal meaning will be applied.

<u>Summary</u>

20. Bringing the above points together, the principles can be summarised as follows[39]:

    a. When interpreting a lease, or any other written contract, the task of the court is to identify the intention of the parties by reference to what a reasonable person, having all the background knowledge which would have been available to

---

[36] See for example *Monsolar IQ Ltd v Woden Park Ltd* [2021] EWCA Civ 961; [2021] L & TR 29 at paragraph 4. In that case, the Court of Appeal held at paragraph 27 that the operation of the principle has not been modified by anything said in *Arnold v Britton.*

[37] See *Monsolar IQ Ltd v Woden Park Ltd* at paragraph 30.

[38] See *Monsolar IQ Ltd v Woden Park Ltd* at paragraphs 31-33.

[39] For a recent summary in the case law, see *ABC Electrification Ltd v Network Rail Infrastructure Ltd* [2020] EWCA Civ 1645 at paragraphs 18-19.

the parties, would have understood them to be using the language in the contract to mean;

b. The court will do so by focussing on the meaning of the relevant words in their documentary, factual and commercial context. That meaning has to be assessed in the light of:

   i. The natural and ordinary meaning of the clause;

   ii. Any other relevant provisions of the contract;

   iii. The overall purpose of the clause and the contract;

   iv. The facts and circumstances known or assumed by the parties at the time that the document was executed;

   v. Commercial common sense;

c. Evidence of prior negotiations[40], or of any party's subjective intentions, is irrelevant;

d. The relevant circumstances are those at the date the agreement was made, not anything that occurred after that date[41];

e. Commercial common sense should not be used to undervalue the importance of the actual words used. Save in an usual case, identifying what the parties meant through the eyes of a reasonable reader is most obviously to be gleaned from the language of the provision;

f. The less clear the words, the more ready the court will be to depart from their natural meaning, but that does not mean

---

40 Which would be relevant in an action for rectification.

41 See for example *Mostyn House Estate Management Company Limited* [2022] EWCA Civ 929 at paragraph 38.

that the court should look for drafting infelicities to facilitate a departure from the natural meaning;

g. Commercial common sense is not to be invoked retrospectively. The mere fact that a contractual arrangement, if interpreted according to its natural language, has worked out badly, or even disastrously, for one of the parties is not a reason for departing from the natural language;

h. Where a lease is required to be protected by registration, extrinsic documents or circumstances which are not publicly accessible will not be given weight in interpreting the lease;

i. Where there is a clear mistake in the language used in a lease, and it is clear what correction ought to be made to correct the mistake, the court may do so as part of the process of construction.

CHAPTER TWO

THE IMPLICATION OF LEASE TERMS AT COMMON LAW

21. Terms can be implied into a contract: (i) in accordance with common law principles relating to business efficacy and/or obviousness; (ii) in accordance with common law principles relating to custom and usage; (iii) in accordance with common law principles relating to the type of contract and (iv) by operation of statute.

22. There has been significant Parliamentary intervention, by means of statutorily implied terms, for alteration and alienation covenants in commercial leases. Those interventions are discussed in chapters 3 and 4. There has been less intervention in the context of user clauses, where it is perhaps more likely that resort will need to be had to the common law principles.

Implication of terms at common law: business efficacy / obviousness

23. At common law, a court may imply a term into a contract where necessary to give effect to the common intention of the parties, judged objectively in light of the express terms of the contract, commercial common sense and the facts known to both parties at the date of the contract. The court will not, however, seek to make or improve the contract for the parties.

24. Case law demonstrates that there are two situations where the implication of a term may be appropriate: (i) where required to give the contract business efficacy and (ii) where the term is so obvious it goes without saying. Some cases have treated these as distinct tests for the implication of a term, others have treated them as different aspects of a single test. On balance, the former approach better

accords with the weight of the case law on the implication of terms, but it will be a rare case where only one test is satisfied and not the other[42].

25. The role of business efficacy in the implication of terms can be seen from the judgment of Bowen LJ in *The Moorcock*[43] where he stated:

"...Now, an implied warranty, or, as it is called, a covenant in law, as distinguished from an express contract or express warranty, really is in all cases founded on the presumed intention of the parties, and upon reason. The implication which the law draws from what must obviously have been the intention of the parties, the law draws with the object of giving efficacy to the transaction and preventing such a failure of consideration as cannot have been within the contemplation of either side; and I believe if one were to take all the cases, and they are many, of implied warranties or covenants in law, it will be found that in all of them the law is raising an implication from the presumed intention of the parties with the object of giving to the transaction such efficacy as both parties must have intended that at all events it should have."

26. As for the role of obviousness, in *Shirlaw v Southern Foundries (1926) Ltd*[44] McKinnon LJ stated that:

"Prima facie that which in any contract is left to be implied and need not be expressed is something so obvious that it goes without saying; so that, if, while the parties were making their bargain, an officious bystander were to suggest some express provision for it in their agreement, they would testily suppress him with a common 'Oh, of course!'"

---

42 *Marks and Spencer plc v BNP Paribas Securities Trust* [2015] UKSC 72; [2016] AC 742; [2015] 3 WLR 1843 at paragraph 21.

43 (1889) 14 PD 64 at 68.

44 [1939] 2 K.B. 206 at 227 (judgment affirmed by the House of Lords at [1940] AC 701).

27. These considerations, which overlap, were applied by Lord Simon in *BP Refinery (Westernport) Pty Ltd v Shire of Hastings*[45] as part of a single test. Giving the majority judgment of the Privy Council, Lord Simon stated:

> *"…[F]or a term to be implied, the following conditions (which may overlap) must be satisfied: (1) it must be reasonable and equitable; (2) it must be necessary to give business efficacy to the contract, so that no term will be implied if the contract is effective without it; (3) it must be so obvious that " it goes without saying"; (4) it must be capable of clear expression; (5) it must not contradict any express term of the contract."*

28. The circumstances in which a court will imply a term into a lease were revisited by the Supreme Court in *Marks and Spencer plc v BNP Paribas Securities Trust*[46], where the relevant principles were reviewed and, in some respects, reformulated[47]. Lord Neuberger, with whom Lords Sumption and Hodge agreed, identified the following principles[48]:

    a) A term will not be implied unless, on an objective assessment of the terms of the contract, it is necessary to give business efficacy to the contract and/or on the basis of the obviousness test. Business necessity and obviousness *"can be alternatives in the sense that only one of them needs to be satisfied"* although in

[45] (1977) 52 ALJR 20 at 26.

[46] [2015] UKSC 72; [2016] AC 742; [2015] 3 WLR 1843, a case which concerned the implication of terms into commercial leases.

[47] In particular, the judgment of Lord Hoffman in *Attorney General of Belize v Belize Telecom Ltd* [2009] UKPC 10; [2009] 1 WLR 1988 (PC); [2009] 2 All ER 1127 was clarified.

[48] See too the helpful summaries of those principles by Hildyard J in *J N Hipwell & Son v Szurek* [2018] L & TR 15 at paragraph 30 and of Lord Hughes in *Ali v Petroleum Company of Trinidad and Tobago* [2017] UKPC 2, [2017] ICR 531 at paragraph 5. For a more recent, detailed, summary of the key principles, see the judgment of Carr LJ in *Yoo Design Services Ltd v Iliv Realty Pte Ltd* [2021] EWCA Civ 560 at paragraph 51.

practice it will be *"a rare case"* where only one of those two requirements is met[49];

b) The test for the implication of a term is necessity, not reasonableness, but *"absolute necessity"* may put the bar too high - it may be more helpful to ask the question whether without the term the contract would lack commercial or practical coherence[50];

c) It is a *"cardinal rule"* that no term can be implied into a contract if it contradicts an express term. When considering whether a term should be implied into a contract on a particular issue, the express words of the contract should first be considered[51];

d) The question whether a term is to be implied is to be judged at the date when the contract is made[52];

e) The implication of a term is not critically dependent on proof of an actual intention of the parties when negotiating the contract. When ascertaining whether there is an implied term, the court should do so by reference to the hypothetical answer of *"notional reasonable people in the position of the parties at the time at which they were contracting"*[53]*;*

f) Where parties have entered into a lengthy and carefully-drafted contract, and omitted to make provision for a particular situation, it will be *"difficult to infer with*

---

49 Paragraph 21.

50 Paragraph 21. Lord Neuberger added that, where a term satisfied the requirements for implication, *"it is hard to think that it would not be reasonable and equitable"*.

51 *Marks and Spencer* paragraph 28.

52 Paragraph 23.

53 Paragraph 21.

confidence" what the parties *"must have intended"*. It is *"tempting, but wrong"* for the court to simply *"fashion a term which will reflect the merits of the situation as they then appear"*. If there are a range of possible terms which could address the situation which has arisen, and it is not clear which would have been preferred, no term can be implied[54];

g) Nor should a term be implied into a detailed commercial contract merely because it appears fair or merely because one considers that the parties would have agreed it if it had been suggested to them. Those are necessary but not sufficient grounds for including a term[55];

h) The court should show restraint when deciding whether to imply terms into a contract[56].

Entire agreement clauses

29. The presence of an entire agreement clause in a lease, while relevant to whether any further terms are to be implied, does not completely preclude them. In *J N Hipwell & Son v Szurek*[57], the Court of Appeal went further, describing as 'entirely correct' a concession made by counsel that *"an entire agreement provision does not affect or prevent the implication of a term to be implied on grounds of business efficacy"*[58]. On the facts, to give business efficacy to the lease, a term was implied that

---

[54] Paragraph 19, quoting from Lord Bingham MR's judgment in *Philips Electronique Grand Public SA v British Sky Broadcasting Ltd* [1995] EMLR 472 at 481–482.

[55] Paragraph 21.

[56] Paragraph 29.

[57] [2018] EWCA Civ 674; [2018] L & TR 15.

[58] Paragraph 27. It is thought that it may go too far to say the presence of an entire agreement clause does not even affect whether to imply a term based on business efficacy.

the landlord would ensure the electrical installation at the premises was safe.

Implication of terms at common law: custom and usage

30. If, in a particular area of for a particular trade, there is an invariable, certain way in which particular words are used, or an invariable, certain custom governing contracts in that area or trade, where the contract is silent, the law will imply that general usage or custom into the contract.[59] As to the general usage of words, this reflects a presumption that *"...the parties did not mean to express in writing the whole of the contract by which they intended to be bound, but a contract with reference to those known usages"*.[60] As to invariable customs, by the presumption *"...the courts are spelling out what both parties know and would, if asked, unhesitatingly agree to be part of the bargain"*.[61] There will be no room for the presumption to operate if the language of the contract, expressly or by implication, is inconsistent with the general usage or custom.[62]

31. Given the variety of ways in which commercial leases deal with alienation, alteration and user, and the impact of market conditions upon the prevailing terms, it is anticipated that this presumption is unlikely to be applicable in this context.

---

[59] See *Hutton v Warren* (1836) 1 M&W 466 at 475.

[60] *Hutton v Warren* (1836) 1 M&W 466 at 475. Likewise, in *Produce Brokers Company, Limited Appellants v Olympia Oil and Cake Company Limited* [1916] 1 AC 314 Lord Atkinson explained, at 324 that: *"If, for instance, in a contract relating to any art or trade or business the parties use terms having technical meanings in that art, trade, or business, then those terms should prima facie have that meaning attributed to them, simply because the parties to the contract presumably used those terms in their technical sense."*

[61] *Liverpool City Council v Irwin* [1977] AC 239 at 253.

[62] See *Produce Brokers Company, Limited Appellants v Olympia Oil and Cake Company Limited* at 324-325.

Implication of terms at common law: relationship of landlord and tenant

32. A court will automatically imply terms into certain classes of agreement, as a necessary incident of the relationship concerned. In the landlord and tenant content, this will include the landlord covenant for quiet enjoyment[63], as well as the landlord obligation not to derogate from grant, both reflecting the general principle that *"a man may not give with one hand and take away with the other"*[64].

33. In the case of the obligation not to derogate from grant, although sometimes put on the basis of being an implied term, the better view is that it arises as an independent rule of law.[65]

34. There is also case law to support the implication of a term that the tenant will act in a 'tenant like manner'[66], although the precise content of that duty and its interrelationship with the express terms of the tenancy are somewhat uncertain. The case law on this is discussed further in chapter 4.

35. Beyond an obligation to act in a tenant like manner, it is considered unlikely that the court would imply any further tenant obligation relating to alienation, alteration or user into a lease on the basis that it was a necessary component of the landlord and tenant relationship, not least because of the wide variety of ways in which commercial leases deal with these issues.

---

63 *Budd-Scott v Daniell* [1902] 2 KB 351 at 358; *Markham v Paget* [1908] 1 Ch 697 at 715-716.

64 *Southwark LBC v Mills* [2001] 1 AC 1 at 23 per Lord Millett, who added that *"there seems to be little if any difference"* in scope between them.

65 *Molton Builders Ltd v Westminster LBC* (1975) 30 P & CR 183 at 186-187.

66 See *Marsden v Edward Heyes Ltd* [1927] 2 KB 1; *Warren v Keen* [1954] 1 QB 15.

Warranties that the premises are fit for a particular use

36. In general, the common law will not imply a term into a lease that the demised premises are fit for any particular use[67] or can be lawfully put to any particular use[68]. The general principle is 'caveat lessee': the tenant takes the premises as they find them.[69]

37. There are exceptions to this principle, including where a dwelling is let furnished and where a landlord retains property which is essential to access the demised premises[70]. Statute has also intervened concerning the condition of residential property.

Summary

38. In summary, the position for implied terms is as follows[71]:

    a) A term will not be implied in a lease unless, on an objective assessment of its terms, it is necessary to give business efficacy to the lease and/or on the basis of the obviousness test;

    b) Business efficacy and obviousness tests are alternative tests. However, it will be a rare case where one, but not the other, is satisfied;

---

67 *Hart v Windsor* (1843) 12 M & W 68 at 87; *Sutton v Temple* (1843) 12 M & W 52; *Bottomley v Bannister* [1932] 1 KB 458 at 468.

68 *Edler v Auerbach* [1950] 1 KB 359 at 368; *Hills v Harris* [1965] 2 QB 601 at 614F-615A; *Molton Builders Ltd v Westminster LBC* (1975) 30 P & CR 183 at 186.

69 This is discussed further in chapter 5.

70 See, in the case of furnished dwellings, *Collins v Hopkins* [1923] 2 KB 617 and in the case of access, *Liverpool CC v Irwin* [1977] AC 239.

71 See the judgment of Carr LJ in *Yoo Design Services Ltd v Iliv Realty Pte Ltd* [2021] EWCA Civ 560 at paragraph 51.

c) The business efficacy test will only be satisfied if, without the term, the contract would lack commercial or practical coherence;

d) The obviousness test will only be met when the implied term is so obvious that it goes without saying. It must be obvious not only that *a* term is to be implied, but precisely what that term is;

e) A term will not be implied if it is inconsistent with an express term of the contract;

f) The implication of a term is not critically dependent on proof of an actual intention of the parties;

g) The question is to be assessed at the time that the contract was made, not with the benefit of hindsight;

h) The equity of a suggested implied term is an essential but not sufficient pre-condition for inclusion. A term should not be implied into a detailed commercial contract merely because it appears fair or merely because the court considers the parties would have agreed it if it had been suggested to them. The test is one of necessity, not reasonableness. That is a stringent test;

i) An entire agreement clause does not prevent the implication of terms;

j) In general, the common law will not imply a term into a lease that the demised premises are fit for any particular use or can be lawfully put to any particular use;

k) The law will imply a term into leases that the landlord will allow the tenant to quietly enjoy the premises;

l) The law will also impose upon the landlord an obligation not to derogate from grant;

m) The law may imply a duty on the tenant to act in a tenant like manner, although the precise scope of such a duty is uncertain.

CHAPTER THREE

RULES GOVERNING ALIENATION COVENANTS

The nature of leasehold ownership / tenant's power to alienate

39. 'Alienable' property is property which may be transferred into new ownership. A lease is alienable property: as a matter of principle, a tenant may assign their interest to somebody else, sublet to another or share possession or occupation of the property. As the Lord Russell of Killowen put it in *Old Grovebury Manor Farm Ltd v W Seymour Plant Sales and Hire Ltd (No 2)*[72], it *"is of the nature of the creation of a term of years that the owner of the term is capable of dealing with it as a piece of property."*

40. Two important consequences flow from this:

    a) If the lease is silent on alienation, the tenant may alienate without the landlord's consent[73]; and

[72] [1979] 1 WLR 1397 at 1399G.

[73] See, in the context of sub-letting, *Leith Properties Ltd. v Byrne* [1983] QB 433 at 439C. See too *Esdaile v Lewis* [1956] 1 WLR 709 at 711 per Jenkins LJ: *"Under a tenancy agreement containing no stipulations regarding subletting the tenant is entitled to sublet in right of his proprietary interest"*. See too *Roberts v Enlayde Ltd* [1924] 1 KB 335 at 338, where Bankes LJ noted that, absent restrictions in the lease, a lessee has *"..the right, as incident to his leasehold estate, to part with the possession of the whole or any part of the premises for the whole or any part of the term."*

b) Even if the lease prohibits alienation, that will not of itself invalidate the assignment[74] or sub-lease[75].

41. So, where a tenant assigns its lease in breach of covenant, the landlord may sue for damages[76] but the assignment will be effective. If the lease contains a forfeiture clause, the landlord may forfeit the lease. Because the unauthorised assignment is effective to vest the remainder of the term in the assignee, the correct recipient of the s146 notice[77] is the assignee, not the assigning tenant.[78]

42. Forfeiture of the lease in the event of an assignment or sub-letting in breach of covenant is not automatic: the landlord must elect to forfeit and first comply with the requirements of s146 of the Law of Property Act 1925[79]. The right to forfeit may also be waived by the landlord, with knowledge of the breach, accepting rent from the assignee or sub-tenant.[80]

---

[74] See *Property & Bloodstock Ltd v Emerton* [1968] 1 Ch 94 at 119E: *"A covenant against assignment of leasehold property does not make an assignment unlawful or ineffective in itself."* See too *Old Grovebury Manor Farm Ltd v W. Seymour Plant Sales and Hire Ltd* (No. 2) [1979] 1 WLR 1397 at 1398G and 1399G.

[75] See *Parker v Jones* [1910] 2 KB 32 at 38: *"A covenant not to underlet without licence does not make an underletting in breach of that covenant illegal; it merely gives the lessor a right to re-enter."*

[76] See *Property & Bloodstock Ltd v Emerton* [1968] 1 Ch 94 at 119F.

[77] The notice required as a precursor to forfeiture: see s146 of the Law of Property Act 1925.

[78] See *Old Grovebury Manor Farm Ltd v W. Seymour Plant Sales and Hire Ltd (No. 2)* [1979] 1 WLR 1397 at 1400F-G.

[79] I.e. the prior service of a notice on the lessee specifying the breach complained of and, if the breach is capable of remedy, requiring the lessee to remedy the breach and the lessee then failing to remedy the breach within a reasonable time thereafter.

[80] In *Hyde v Pimley* [1952] 2 QB 506, the court went further and found that, in addition to waiving the right to forfeit, the acceptance of rent for four and

43. Where a party knowingly and intentionally induces the tenant to breach their lease, by assigning the lease or granting a sub-tenancy in breach of covenant, without reasonable justification or excuse, that party commits the tort of inducing breach of contract[81]. In such a case, the court has jurisdiction to order the reassignment of the lease or the surrender of the sub-lease.[82]

44. An assignment or sub-letting will still need to comply with the applicable formalities for the creation of interests in land.[83] Where an intended sub-letting or assignment fails for want of compliance with formalities, the covenant against sub-letting/assigning will not have been breached as there will have been no assignment/sub-letting.[84]

The interpretation of covenants against alienation / identifying the scope of the restriction

45. The principles which govern the interpretation of leases generally have been set out in chapter 1. In the context of alienation clauses, it

---

a half months with knowledge of the sub-letting amounted to an implied consent to the transaction: see 512-513.

81 As to the ingredients of this tort, see *OBG Ltd v Allan* [2007] UKHL 21; [2008] 1 AC 1 at paragraphs 39–44 (Lord Hoffman) and 168–193 (Lord Nicholls). For a more recent discussion of the required mental state of the tortfeasor, see *Allen v Pollock* [2020] EWCA Civ 258; [2020] QB 781 at paragraphs 11 to 37.

82 See *Esso Petroleum Co Ltd v Kingswood Motors (Addlestone) Ltd* [1974] QB 142 at 156-157; *Hemingway Securities Ltd v Dunraven Ltd* (1996) 71 P. & C.R. 30 at 32-33.

83 For example, s2 of the Law of Property (Miscellaneous Provisions) Act 1989, s52-53 of the Law of Property Act 1925. However, where an assignment is made in writing and complies with the requirements of s2 of the 1989 Act, but not by deed so as not to transfer the legal estate, it may nonetheless operate as an agreement to assign so as to vest an equitable interest in the assignee.

84 See *Old Grovebury Manor Farm Ltd v W. Seymour Plant Sales and Hire Ltd (No. 2)* [1979] 1 WLR 1397 at 1399H.

is important to pay close attention to the precise wording of the restriction. The technical distinctions between legal and equitable interests, and between assigning, sub-letting, sharing possession, sharing occupation etc, have been respected by the courts in interpreting the scope of such covenants. The distinction between obligations relating to (1) the premises as a whole, and only as a whole and (2) the whole and/or any part of them is likewise important.

Covenants not to assign

46. A covenant 'not to assign' is only broken by a legal assignment of the entire residue of the term, it is not broken by an equitable assignment of the premises or by a declaration of trust of the premises in favour of a third party[85]. A covenant 'not to assign or part with the possession' of premises would, however, be broken by an equitable assignment where the assignee is allowed into possession.

Covenants not to part with possession

47. The question whether there has been a parting with possession in any given case will depend upon all the facts and circumstances[86]. In answering that question, the courts have tended to give the word 'possession' its technical legal meaning and to uphold the distinction between a person being in 'possession' of premises and being in 'occupation' of them (albeit the distinction has been described as *"somewhat elusive and not entirely easy to define"*[87]).

48. A person will be in possession of premises if able to exercise the rights of an owner in relation to it, even if only temporarily and subject to certain restrictions[88], such as deciding who may be admitted to the

---

85 See *Gentle v Faulkner* [1900] 2 QB 267 at 274 (per A.J. Smith LJ) and 276-277 (per Romer LJ).

86 *Lam Kee Ying Sdn Bhd v Lam Shes Tong* [1975] AC 247 at 256.

87 *Akici v LR Butlin Ltd* [2005] EWCA Civ 1296; [2006] 1 WLR 201 at paragraph 39.

88 *Street v Mountford* [1985] 1 AC 809 at 816B-C.

premises and being able to exclude their landlord unless the landlord is exercising reserved rights. In other words, the concept of legal possession is tied to the control of premises.[89]

49. It is the grant of exclusive possession for a term at a rent which is the hallmark of a lease, as opposed to a licence.[90] The words used by the parties ('lease' or 'licence') are not determinative in ascertaining the nature of the agreement, what matters is whether the conduct of the parties show that what was intended was that the occupier should be granted exclusive possession at a rent for a term. If so, a tenancy will have been created, regardless of whether or not the agreement is expressed to be licence.[91]

50. Case law establishes that the obligation not to part with possession of premises:

    a) Will be breached by an assignment of them[92];

    b) Will be breached by granting an underlease of the premises for part of the term[93];

---

[89] See for example *Akici v LR Butlin Ltd* [2005] EWCA Civ 1296; [2006] 1 WLR 201 at paragraph 46.

[90] Whilst in exceptional circumstances there can be exclusive possession and yet no lease, such cases are rare (for example, where there was no intention to create legal relations, and the occupation was referable to an act of charity). As the Court of Appeal put it in *Nunn v Dalrymple* (1989) 21 HLR 569 at 578: *"prima facie, where you have exclusive occupation coupled with the payment of rent, then the relationship is that of landlord and tenant and is not a relationship of licensee."* While the payment of rent is a hallmark of a tenancy, unlike exclusive possession, it is not an essential requirement: *Ashburn Anstalt v Arnold* [1989] Ch 1.

[91] *Street v Mountford* [1985] 1 AC 809 at 821C-D.

[92] *Marks v Warren* [1979] 1 All ER 29 at 30g to 31a.

[93] As, by the underlease, the tenant is granted exclusive possession of the premises.

c) Is unlikely to be breached by the grant of a licence[94];

d) Will not be breached by the lessee parting with possession of only part of the premises[95]. Careful drafting of a lease, providing that references to the premises are to include any part of them, will avoid this difficulty;

e) Will not be breached by the lessee sharing possession. For example, in *Jackson v Simons*[96], a tenant granted a neighbouring nightclub a licence between fixed hours to use part of the demised premises for the sale of tickets. Romer J held that:

   i. The licence granted did not amount to an underletting so as to have created an interest in land, all that was conferred was *"a mere privilege or licence to use a part of the demised premises"*[97];

   ii. As was admitted, the particular acts done *"amounted to a sharing of the possession of part of the demised premises"*[98];

---

[94] Because the rights of the licensee are likely to fall short of the degree of control which constitutes possession.

[95] In *Church v Brown* (1808) 15 Ves 258, Lord Eldon remarked at 265 that a covenant *"not to part with the possession of the premises"* would *"not have restrained the tenant from parting with a part of the premises"*. This statement was quoted approvingly by the Joyce J in *Grove v Portal* [1902] 1 Ch 727 at 731.

[96] [1923] 1 Ch 373.

[97] At 380.

[98] At 380.

iii. However, the defendant lessee retained the legal possession of the whole of the premises at all material times[99];

iv. A lessee *"who retains such possession does not commit a breach of a covenant against parting with possession by allowing other people to use the premises"*[100].

f) Will not be breached by the lessee sharing occupation[101].

Covenants against sharing possession

51. The Court of Appeal helpfully explained the nature of shared possession in *Akici v LR Butlin Ltd*[102]. The court began by considering the comments of Sir Douglas Frank QC in *Tulapam Properties Ltd v De Almeida*[103], where the Deputy Judge gave an expanded meaning to a covenant against 'sharing possession', to encompass sharing occupation, on the basis that to do otherwise would strip the obligation of any content. This was on the basis that possession is unitary and cannot be shared, the Deputy Judge stating that:

"That the use of the premises has been shared…is beyond dispute. The office use of the basement and first floor and probably the upper floors has been shared. Does that amount to a sharing of possession? In a strict legal sense the word "possession" has a highly technical meaning, and the sharing of possession is an unknown concept. It has been said that a possession is single and indivisible. So when you get what might be termed

99 At 380.

100 At 380.

101 *Lam Kee Ying Sdn Bhd v Lam Shes Tong* [1975] AC 247 at 255f to 256c. See too *Akici v LR Butlin Ltd* [2005] EWCA Civ 1296; [2006] 1 WLR 201 at paragraph 25.

102 [2005] EWCA Civ 1296; [2006] 1 WLR 201.

103 [1981] 2 EGLR 55.

a sharing of possession, the two sharers become one as, say, joint tenants, and one is back to the original concept. But "possession" also has a broader popular meaning, and it means the sharing of the use or occupation.

It falls to the court if possible to give a meaning to the expression in the lease rather than to say that it can have no meaning, because clearly the words would not be there unless they were intended to have a meaning. Nor should the court rest on the easy pillow of uncertainty. I think that sharing possession here means, and would have been taken by the parties to mean, sharing the use of these premises with somebody else. What the plaintiffs, as landlords, must have been concerned with was that there should not be what is commonly called multi-occupation, as occurred here. In my judgment, there was and is a breach of that covenant."[104]

52. In *Ackici*, the Court of Appeal held this aspect of *Tulapam Properties Ltd* to be wrongly decided. Neuberger LJ, giving the judgment of the court, did not accept that possession cannot be shared[105] and explained that where a tenant shares possession of premises with another, while the possession of the premises would indeed become *"joint and, in a sense, therefore unitary"*[106], as *"a matter of ordinary language, a lessee who lets another person into possession of the demised premises, so that they are both in possession, can properly be said to "share" possession with that other person"*. Neuberger LJ therefore did not agree with Sir Douglas Frank QC that to give the word 'possession' its usual meaning in the context of a covenant not to share possession would deprive the covenant of any legal effect[107]. The effect of such a covenant, with possession given its technical meaning, is to *"prevent the conversion of a tenancy to a single lessee into what, in practical terms, will amount to a joint tenancy."*[108] In a covenant against sharing

[104] At 56.

[105] At paragraph 28.

[106] Paragraph 28.

[107] Paragraph 29.

[108] Paragraph 29.

possession, 'possession' should therefore be given its technical legal meaning[109].

53. Whether a tenant is (1) only sharing occupation with another or (2) has permitted them a degree of control over the premises which amounts to sharing possession will depend upon the particular circumstances[110].

Covenants against underletting

54. A covenant against underletting premises will not be broken by the grant of a licence. The covenant is breached when the lessee, by the grant of the underlease, parts with exclusive possession of the premises.

55. If the covenant is worded so as to be limited to the whole of premises, the grant of an underlease of part only will not breach the covenant.[111] Where the covenant, read in the context of the lease as a whole, does not specify whether it applies (1) only to the premises as a whole or (2) to any part of them, the former construction is likely to be preferred. For example, proceeding on the basis that covenants against alienation are to be interpreted strictly:

   a) In *Cook v Shoesmith*, the lease provided that: *"I hereby agree to rent the above house as from July 15, 1944, at the rate of 65l. per annum exclusive of rates payable in advance on Saturday of each and every week in the sum of 1l. 5s. and I further agree not to sublet."* The Court of Appeal interpreted the restriction on

---

[109] Paragraph 30, subject to the lease containing positive indications that some other meaning was intended.

[110] See *Akici v LR Butlin Ltd* [2005] EWCA Civ 1296; [2006] 1 WLR 201 paragraph 38.

[111] See *Cook v Shoesmith* [1951] 1 KB 752, applying the dictum of Lord Eldon in *Church v. Brown (1808) 15 Ves 258* at 265.

subletting as prohibiting the subletting of the whole house only, not a subletting of part[112];

b) In *Esdaile v Lewis*[113], the lease provided for *"No subletting allowed without the written consent of the landlord"*. The majority of the Court of Appeal held that the restriction would only be breached by a subletting of the whole, not a subletting of part.[114]

56. A covenant against underletting 'any part' of the premises will be breached by an underletting of the whole of the premises, as the restriction encompasses transactions by which every part is underlet[115].

57. Where a covenant precludes underletting the whole of the premises other than on certain conditions, and part of the premises is underlet in compliance with those conditions and part is not, whether the covenant is breached will turn upon the particular circumstances and the drafting of the conditions. For example:

a) Where a covenant was not to underlet the whole of the premises without the lessor's consent, and the lessee underlet part of the premises with consent and then the remaining part without consent, the covenant was breached as the lessee

---

[112] [1951] 1 KB 752 at 754-756.

[113] [1956] 1 WLR 709; [1956] 2 All ER 357.

[114] [1956] 1 WLR 709 - see the judgment of Jenkins LJ at 712 and Hodson LJ at 712-713.

[115] See *Field v Barkworth* [1986] 1 WLR 137 at 139F-G, where Nicholls J explained that *"...if after an assignment or underletting of the whole of the premises one asked the question: "Has there been an assignment or underletting of any part of the premises?", the answer plainly would be "Yes." The answer would be yes, because what had been assigned or underlet would be every part of the premises and this covenant against assignment or underletting of any part of the premises in my view plainly embraces the assignment or underletting of every part."*

never obtained the lessor's consent to the underletting of the whole[116]; but

b) Where the covenant provided that the lessee was not to underlet the whole of the premises without consent, but that no consent was required for an underletting of the premises for a term not exceeding three years, and the lessee sublet a portion of the premises on a weekly tenancy, and then sublet the remainder of the premises on a 21-year tenancy, the covenant was not breached. This was because the lessee had not underlet the whole of premises for a term exceeding three years without consent, which is what the covenant prohibited[117].

Covenants against sharing occupation

58. Whether there is a sharing of occupation in any given case is highly fact dependent. As was noted by Lord Nicholls in *Graysim Holdings Ltd v P & O Property Holdings Ltd*[118]: "*... the concept of occupation is not a legal term of art, with one single and precise meaning applicable in all circumstances. Its meaning varies according to the subject matter.*" Where there is a 'sharing', whether a tenant is (1) only sharing occupation with another or (2) has permitted them a degree of control over the premises which amounts to sharing possession will likewise depend upon the particular circumstances[119].

59. In *Mean Fiddler Holdings Ltd v Islington London Borough Council*[120], the Court of Appeal considered a case where the lessee of a nightclub

---

[116] *Chatterton v Terrell* [1923] AC 578, see in particular 582 and 585.

[117] *Roberts v Enlayde Ltd* [1924] 1 KB 335 at 339, per Scrutton LJ. See too the judgment of Atkin LJ at 340.

[118] [1996] 1 AC 329 at 334G.

[119] See *Akici v LR Butlin Ltd* [2005] EWCA Civ 1296; [2006] 1 WLR 201 paragraph 38.

[120] [2003] EWCA Civ 160; (2003) 2 P & CR 7.

had offered the club to external promoters who would stage club nights, which included taking full responsibility for admission revenues, advertising revenue and administration. The lessor argued there had been a breach of the covenant against sharing occupation. Upholding the judgment below that the covenant had not been breached, the Court of Appeal declined to lay down detailed guidance for determining when a covenant against sharing occupation will be breached. Carnwath LJ considered the question to be one of *"mixed fact and law – where there is no precise test"*[121]. Emphasising that such matters have to be looked at in a common-sense way[122], the court found no error of law in the trial judge's decision that there was no sharing of occupation because the lessee remained *"exclusively responsible for everything concerned with the property as opposed to the event"*.[123]

60. Lord Carnwath gave, as an example of an arrangement which would not breach the covenant, the situation where a disc jockey takes over the stage and uses a dressing room, even if a regular visitor and given a key to the dressing room.[124]

61. On the particular facts, Sir Christopher Staughton considered the test to be whether the promoter was *"operating a separate business on the premises from that carried on by the tenant"*[125]. He added that, if the tenant is carrying on a business and the promoter participates in that business under the landlord's supervision and control, there is not a sharing of occupation.[126]

[121] Paragraph 30.

[122] Paragraph 32.

[123] Paragraphs 35-36.

[124] Paragraph 32.

[125] Paragraph 41.

[126] Paragraph 41.

Scope for an expansive interpretation of alienation covenants / implication of alienation covenants

62. There is a long line of case law which supports interpreting alienation covenants strictly[127], giving effect to the technical distinctions between legal and equitable interests and between assigning, sub-letting, sharing possession, sharing occupation etc. Further, unless a covenant is expressed to apply to 'all or part' of demised premises, restrictions on underletting etc. have been construed as applying to the whole of the premises only.[128]

63. The rationale for this strict approach is that a lease bestows on the lessee a piece of property and their rights in respect of it *"are not to be cut down except by clear words"*[129]. In *Marks v Warren*[130], Browne-Wilkinson J explained that *"if a landlord wishes to restrict the free alienation by his tenant of the estate that has been granted to him, the burden lies on the landlord to express that restriction in clear terms, so that there can be no doubt as to what the restriction consists of, especially as the penalty for a breach is forfeiture."*[131]

64. Given this, it is considered that there is little scope for landlords to seek to expand the meaning of alienation clauses through interpretation. Likewise, there is little scope for seeking to bring in additional restrictions on alienation thought the implication of

---

[127] *Church v Brown* (1808) 15 Ves 258 at 265: "*...these covenants having been always construed by Courts of Law with the utmost jealousy to prevent the restraint from going beyond the express stipulation*", *Grove v Portal* [1902] 1 Ch 727 at 731, *Cook v Shoesmith* [1951] 1 KB 752 at 754-755, *Marks v Warren* [1979] 1 All ER 29 at 30h, *Lam Kee Ying Sdn Bhd v Lam Shes Tong* [1975] AC 247 (PC) at 256C.

[128] *Cook v Shoesmith* [1951] 1 KB 752 at 754-756; *Esdaile v Lewis* [1956] 1 WLR 709 at 712-713.

[129] *Cook v Shoesmith* [1951] 1 KB 752 at 755.

[130] [1979] 1 All ER 29.

[131] 30h. The same point was made by the Privy Council in *Lam Kee Ying Sdn Bhd v Lam Shes Tong* [1975] AC 247 (PC) at 256C.

terms. Given that, save for any limitations agreed by the lessor and lessee, the nature of a lease is that it is alienable property, it is hard to envisage circumstances in which restrictions on alienation can be said to necessary to give a lease business efficacy or to be so obvious that they go without saying. Given the variety of alienation covenants that exist, nor would it be easy for a landlord to show not just that restrictions on alienation generally were intended but that a specific form of restriction was intended.

65. This strict approach has led to results which have caused the courts concern, particular the principle that, save where express words are used, restrictions on parting with possession/underletting only apply to the premises as a whole and do not catch transactions by which there is a parting with possession of part only, or an underletting of part only. For example, in *Esdaile v Lewis*[132], the lease provided for *"No subletting allowed without the written consent of the landlord"* and the majority of the court felt it was bound by authority to construe the restriction as preventing only subletting of the whole, not of part.[133]

66. This conclusion was not reached with any enthusiasm. While Jenkins LJ thought it right that *"it behoves a landlord who is seeking to cut down the rights prima facie conferred on his tenant by the letting to express in clear words the extent to which those rights are intended to be cut down"*[134], he confessed that, free from authority, he would have found that the words 'no subletting allowed' meant *"that there was to be no subletting at all in relation to the premises, whether in whole or in part"*[135]. However, the judge held that *"Whatever one may think of the*

[132] [1956] 1 WLR 709.

[133] [1956] 1 WLR 709 - see the judgment of Jenkins LJ at 712 and Hodson LJ at 712-713.

[134] 711.

[135] 710.

principle which the cases establish, it is an established principle for better or for worse"[136].

67. Hodson LJ likewise noted that free from authority he would have interpreted the restriction as prohibiting the subletting of any part of the premises in question, but that he considered the court was constrained by authority to construe the covenant as preventing only a subletting of the whole[137].

68. Danckwerts J dissented and held that the covenant was *"perfectly clear"* and that 'no sub-letting allowed' *"is a perfectly plain expression which means…exactly what it says, that there is to be no subletting whatever, and that therefore there must be no subletting of a part of the premises any more than of the whole premises. There simply must be no subletting"*[138].

69. The cases which establish that alienation clauses should be interpreted strictly and that a restriction is limited to the whole unless expressly stated otherwise pre-date the modern case law on the correct approach to interpretation[139]. As Neuberger LJ noted in *Akici v LR Butlin Ltd*[140], the approach evident in those cases *"…may well be a little less powerful than it was 30 years ago on the basis that such canons of construction are now given rather less weight"*[141].

70. It may be then that there is now a little more scope to argue against strict constructions of alienation clauses which lead to results which

---

136 712.

137 712.

138 714.

139 For an account of the modern approach to interpretation, see the discussion in chapter 1.

140 [2005] EWCA Civ 1296; [2006] 1 WLR 201.

141 Paragraph 30.

sit awkwardly with the language used. *Esdaile v Lewis* is, perhaps, one case where the opposite result might now be reached.

71. That said, it is considered that for the most part the courts are likely to continue with the strict approach evident in the older cases. The rationale for the strict approach that a landlord who wishes to diminish their tenant's rights must do so in clear terms is likely to continue to be given weight by the courts, particularly where a breach of covenant subjects the tenant to the risk of forfeiture. In *Akici*, whist recognising that cannons of construction are no longer given the weight they once were, Neuberger LJ nevertheless considered that in that case: *"...the modern approach, namely that such covenants should be given what is, in their documentary, factual and commercial context, their natural and commercially sensible meaning, indicates, in my judgment, the same result."*[142]

72. Particularly where a lease has been professionally drafted, with detailed provisions on which forms of alienation are restricted, it is considered that the courts will, in substance, continue to apply the strict approach evident in the older cases.

Common forms of alienation covenant

73. Because of the technical distinctions discussed above, most well drafted commercial leases include covenants restricting assigning, underletting or parting with/sharing possession of the whole or part of the demised premises, as well as against allowing other persons into occupation of the whole or part of the premises and sharing occupation of the premises.

Involuntary assignments

74. Covenants against assignment are, when worded in general terms, likely to be interpreted as prohibiting voluntary assignments but not

[142] Paragraph 30.

extending to involuntary assignments by operation of law[143]. So, for example, where a lease vests in a trustee in bankruptcy by operation of law, a covenant not to assign the property without consent will not be breached.

Assignments by trustees in bankruptcy

75. Where a lease vests in a trustee in bankruptcy who then assigns the lease onward, where the alienation covenant is worded in general terms the covenant is unlikely to be breached[144]. Various reasons have been offered for this.

76. In *Doe v. Bevan*[145], the covenant was that *"the tenant, his executors, administrators, or assigns, should not assign...without the consent in writing of the lessor"*. It was held by the court that an assignment by the trustee in bankruptcy did not breach the covenant. Delivering one of the three judgments of the court, Bayley J held that:

"All that has followed upon his bankruptcy is not by his act but by the operation of law, transferring his property to his assignees. Then shall the assignees have capacity to take it, and yet not to dispose of it? Shall they take it only for their own benefit, or be obliged to retain it in their hands to the prejudice of the creditors, for whose benefit the law originally cast it upon them? Undoubtedly that can never be. They must, therefore, have a power to sell for the purposes for which it was given them..."

77. Subsequent cases have taken a narrower view of the applicable principle. In *Re Birkbeck Permanent Benefit Building Society*, referring back to *Doe v. Bevan*, the true principle was expressed to be that *"...prima facie a contractual restriction of assignment does not apply to*

143 *Doe v. Bevan* (1815) 3 M & S 353 at 360-361.

144 *Doe v. Bevan* (1815) 3 M & S 353 at 360-361.

145 (1815) 3 M & S 353.

the assignment by a person on whom the property has devolved by operation of law, and who is under an obligation to assign."[146]

78. Later, in *Re Farrows Bank Ltd*[147], considering the *Doe v. Bevan* line of case law, Lord Sterndale M.R. considered that:

"The real question which arose in the bankruptcy cases to which we have been referred may be stated in this way. There was a covenant that the lessee should not assign without the consent of the lessor, and that bound him and his assigns. The trustee in bankruptcy had assigned without the consent of the lessor. Was that an act of the lessee or his assigns? It was not of course necessary to hold that the assignment was not his act; that was obvious on the face of it; and what was held was that the trustee in bankruptcy was not the assign of the bankrupt within the meaning of the covenant, because the covenant related only to voluntary assigns and not to assigns in law. That is really the basis of all those decisions, whatever may have been the language used."[148]

79. In *Re Wright*[149], the court returned to this line of case law. Noting that while the language used by the judges in *Doe v Bevan "might be construed in a wide sense"*, the *"real basis of the decision"* was held to be that:

"... involuntary assigns, such as a trustee in bankruptcy, or the commissioners for the purpose of distributing bankrupts' property, as it was in that actual case, are not assigns within the meaning of such a covenant and are, therefore, not prohibited from parting with or assigning the leasehold property in question"[150].

---

146 [1913] 2 Ch 34 at 38.

147 [1921] 2 Ch 164.

148 [1921] 2 Ch 164 at 174-175.

149 [1949] Ch 729.

150 [1949] Ch 729 at 735.

80. The court in *Re Wright* concluded that:

a) *"...all that cases like Doe v. Bevan (i) have decided is that the trustee in bankruptcy is not an assign within the covenant that the lessee or his assigns shall not dispose of the property"*[151];

b) Where the words of a covenant are different, they are capable of effectively prohibiting assignments by trustees in bankruptcy. In *Re Wright*, the obligation not to assign without the consent of the landlord was expressed as applying to the tenant and their successors in title. Danckwerts J was *"...unable to see why a trustee in bankruptcy, even though he obtains the property by operation of law, is not a successor in title of the bankrupt, that is to say, the tenant"*[152]. The trustee in bankruptcy was accordingly bound by the terms of the covenant.

Assignments by liquidators

81. Where a lessee enters into voluntary[153] or compulsory[154] liquidation, because the liquidator acts on the behalf of the company, and any assignment is made by the company itself, any covenant against assignment will apply. In *Re Farrows Bank Ltd*[155], the tenant, whose lease contained a covenant not to assign without the lessor's consent, was placed into compulsory liquidation and the liquidator sought a declaration that they could assign without the lessor's consent. Overturning the first instance decision to grant the declaration, Lord Sterndale M.R. held that:

[151] At 736.

[152] At 736.

[153] As to which, see *Cohen v Popular Restaurants Ltd* [1917] 1 KB 480.

[154] As to which, see *Re Farrows Bank Ltd* [1921] 2 Ch 164.

[155] [1921] 2 Ch 164.

"The assignment would be made by the liquidator acting on behalf of the company. It would therefore be an assignment by the company itself, and if made without the consent of the lessor, it would, in my opinion, be as plain a breach of the covenant as could possibly be..."[156]

82. As for the *Doe v. Bevan* line of cases, as then understood, Younger LJ accepted those cases were *"somewhat analogous"* but considered them to be *"based on no very intelligible principle"* and stated he was *"not disposed to extend"* them.[157] As explained above, Lord Sterndale M.R. explained *Doe v Bevan* on the basis that the trustee in bankruptcy was not an assign of the tenant within the meaning of the particular covenant, because the covenant related only to voluntary assigns and not to assigns in law, and so was not subject to the obligation not to assign without the lessor's consent. As above, *Re Wright* has confirmed that the opposite result can be reached by suitable drafting.

Express provision for assignments by trustees in bankruptcy / forfeiture clauses triggered by bankruptcy or liquidation

83. It was held by Lord Ellenborough C.J. in *Doe v. Bevan*[158] to be a point *"long settled"* that in *"extraordinary cases, such as the bankruptcy of his tenant"*, a landlord may *"restrain the alienation by an express proviso"*. The ability of lessors to do so, by suitable drafting, was reaffirmed in *Re Wright*[159]. Accordingly, many modern commercial leases are drafted to expressly prohibit involuntary assignments or assignments by operation of law.

---

156 At 174. Similar reasons were given by Warrington LJ at 176-176 and by Younger LJ at 177.

157 177-178.

158 (1815) 3 M & S 353 at 357.

159 [1949] Ch 729.

84. Lessors can also be protected by making provision for forfeiture in the event of a lessee's bankruptcy or liquidation. Such clauses are commonplace and have been upheld by the courts.[160]

Absolute covenants against alienation

85. An absolute covenant outright prohibits any alienation, rather than prohibiting alienation save in specified circumstances. Where there is an absolute covenant, the landlord remains free if it wishes to waive the covenant for specific transactions but is under no legal obligation to do so. Given the absolute prohibition, the landlord is not required to behave reasonably in deciding whether or not the waive the prohibition, nor to given reasons if it decides not to do so.

86. Given these consequences, the argument has been made that because a landlord can waive an absolute covenant, the prohibition in such a covenant is, in substance, a prohibition not to do the prohibited act without licence or consent, so as to bring the covenant within the scope of s19 of the Landlord and Tenant Act 1927[161]. In the current context, s19(1) imports into covenants not to alienate without the consent of the landlord a requirement that such consent is not to be unreasonably withheld.

87. Although this possibility of s19(1) applying to absolute covenants against alienation was left open in *Property & Bloodstock Ltd v Emerton*[162], it is considered that the better view is that s19(1) has no application to such covenants. Section 19(1) is limited covenants which are prohibit alienation *"without licence or consent"*. As recognised by Court of Appeal in *F. W. Woolworth and Company Ltd*

[160] See, for example, *Civil Service Co-operative Society Ltd v Trustee of Sir J R D McGrigor* [1923] 2 Ch 347 at 354-355. The validity of such clauses is also acknowledged by the statutory regulation of them: see s146(9)-(10) of the Law of Property Act 1925.

[161] The workings of which are discussed below.

[162] [1968] 1 Ch 94 at 119G-120A.

v Lambert[163] *"…although of course it is true that every covenant can be released by the landlord if he so thinks fit"*, long before s19 came into force, *"the difference between an absolute covenant not to assign and a covenant not to assign without the licence or consent of the landlord, was well recognised"* and a finding that s19(1) is appliable to absolute covenants *"would be to disregard the words of the section altogether—namely, the words 'without licence or consent.'"*[164]

88. The same analysis applies to the applicability of s144 of the Law of Property Act 1925 to absolute covenants, which is likewise limited to covenants against assigning etc[165] *"without licence or consent"*.

89. It is considered that few well advised tenants would agree to take on a lengthy lease containing an absolute prohibition against assignment. Such a prohibition is likely to have a significant impact the level of the rent achievable, as well as on the rent determined in any rent review.

<u>Qualified covenants against alienation</u>

90. A qualified covenant against alienation does not outright prohibit alienation, but prohibits it save where specified conditions are met, the most common being the prior consent of the landlord being obtained. It is helpful to distinguish between two forms of qualified covenant:

    a) Partially qualified covenants, where alienation is prohibited without the consent of the landlord;

---

[163] [1937] Ch 37.

[164] See 58-59.

[165] The section is applicable to *"all leases containing a covenant, condition, or agreement against assigning, underletting, or parting with the possession, or disposing of the land or property leased without licence or consent"*.

b) Fully qualified covenants, where alienation is prohibited without the consent of the landlord, such consent not to be unreasonably withheld.

91. Subject to the statutory interventions discussed below, it is a matter for the parties what limitations to place upon a landlord's ability to refuse consent to alienation. Parties can, if they choose, go further in restricting the landlord's latitude to refuse than is provided for by statute.

92. Qualified alienation covenants have been the subject of significant statutory interventions which will be considered in turn.

Law of Property Act 1925 section 144: prohibition on landlords taking a fine as a condition of consenting to an assignment, underletting, parting with possession or disposal of leased property

93. By s144 of the LPA 1925, in all leases *"containing a covenant, condition, or agreement against assigning, underletting, or parting with the possession, or disposing of the land or property leased without licence or consent"*, unless the lease contains an express provision to the contrary, the covenant is deemed to be subject to a proviso that *"no fine or sum of money in the nature of a fine shall be payable for or in respect of such licence or consent"*. The section continues that this proviso *"...does not preclude the right to require the payment of a reasonable sum in respect of any legal or other expense incurred in relation to such licence or consent."*[166]

[166] In *Goldman v Abbott* [1989] 48 EG 151, the Court of Appeal left unresolved whether s144 confers on landlords a right to recover reasonable expenses even if no licence or consent is granted. Kerr LJ did not think that *"one can conclude with confidence that the latter part of that provision is necessarily confined to cases in which a licence or consent is in fact granted"*, though suspected that expect practitioners would take that view.

94. Section 144 states expressly that the deemed proviso will apply unless the lease contains an express provision to the contrary – it is therefore possible to contract out of the s144 protection.

95. 'Fine' is defined by s205(1)(xxiii) of the LPA 1925. The definition is a broad one, providing that a fine includes *"a premium or foregift and any payment, consideration, or benefit in the nature of a fine, premium or foregift"*. Case law has likewise emphasised the broad scope of 'fine'. For example, in *Gardner v Cone*[167] the landlord, a brewer, consented to the assignment of the lease of a free public house on the condition that for the remainder of the term the lease was to be a tied public house. The court concluded the word 'fine' in s144 should be given *"a wide meaning"* which included *"the benefit conferred by a stipulation for the giving of a tie in the case of a public house"*[168].

Landlord and Tenant Act 1927 section 19(1)(a): requirement that a landlord's consent to an assignment, underletting, charging or parting with possession must not be unreasonably withheld

96. Section 19(1)(a) of the LTA 1927 provides that:

> *"(1) In all leases whether made before or after the commencement of this Act containing a covenant condition or agreement against assigning, underletting, charging or parting with the possession of demised premises or any part thereof without licence or consent, such covenant condition or agreement shall, notwithstanding any express provision to the contrary, be deemed to be subject—*
>
>> *(a) to a proviso to the effect that such licence or consent is not to be unreasonably withheld, but this proviso does not preclude the right of the landlord to require payment of a reasonable sum in respect of any legal or other expenses incurred in connection with such licence or consent…"*

[167] [1928] Ch 955.

[168] At 964.

97. Section 19(1)(a) has the effect of writing additional words into the alienation covenant[169]. It has the effect of upgrading a partially qualified covenant into a fully qualified covenant. Unlike s144 of the LPA 1925, the operation of s19(1)(a) cannot be excluded by agreement[170].

98. Section 19(1)(a) can, however, be avoided by the use of an absolute covenant: such a restriction is not a covenant against assigning 'without licence or consent' and so s19(1)(a) will not apply to it.

99. Section 19(1)(a) may also not apply where a covenant goes further in restricting the landlord than an obligation not to unreasonably refuse consent. For example, in *Moat v Martin*[171], the covenant provided that the tenant was "*not to assign underlet or part with possession of the demised premises or any part thereof without the consent in writing of the landlord such consent will not be withheld in the case of a respectable and responsible person ....*". The Court of Appeal held that, where the proposed assignment was to a respectable and responsible person, the landlord had no discretion at all to refuse consent, whether it would be reasonable to do so or not, such that s19(1)(a) was inapplicable.[172]

---

169 A point made by Greene LJ in *F. W. Woolworth and Company, Limited v Lambert* [1937] Ch 37 at 60.

170 Section 19(1)(a) stating it applies "*notwithstanding any express provision to the contrary*".

171 [1950] 1 KB 175.

172 See 180-181 (Evershed MR), who considered that where there was an assignment to a respectable and responsible person *"no consent was required or (which comes to the same thing)"* that the effect of the covenant was that *"[the landlord] would not in any circumstances withhold his consent"*. Denning LJ (at 181) held that the landlord's consent was still required, but that because the restriction on the landlord's discretion went further than limiting them to acting reasonably, it was not a restriction 'to the contrary' disapplied by s19(1)(a) and should therefore be given effect. Hodson J (at 181) considered that, for an assignment to a respectable and responsible person, there was no room for consent to *"be withheld at all"*, such that there

100. For qualified covenants which are subject to s19(1)(a), where there are no reasonable grounds upon which a landlord could refuse consent to an assignment, the tenant must still seek the landlord's consent and it will be a breach of covenant not to do so.[173]

101. A lease may permissibly restrict a tenant's ability to apply for a licence to assign etc. by making it conditional upon compliance with conditions precedent. This does not fall foul of the anti-avoidance provisions in s19[174].

102. By s19(4), s19(1)(a) and does not apply to certain agricultural leases[175].

Landlord and Tenant Act 1927 section 19(1)(b): removal of the requirement to seek consent to an assignment, underletting, charging or parting with possession in building leases

103. Section 19(1)(b) makes provision for building leases, specifically leases for a term of more than forty years made in consideration wholly or partly of the erection, or the substantial improvement, addition or alteration of buildings. Where such a lease contains a covenant against assigning, underletting or parting with possession

---

was *"no room to inquire whether the consent is being withheld reasonably or unreasonably"* and s19(1) did not apply.

173 See *Eastern Telegraph Co Ltd v Dent* [1899] 1 QB 835. There, the lease provided that it was not be assigned without consent, and that such consent was not to be unreasonably withheld. The tenant assigned the lease without asking for consent, to a firm to which *"no possible objection"* could have been taken. The Court of Appeal nevertheless confirmed that the assignment was in breach of covenant, as no consent was sought.

174 See *Bocardo v S&M Hotels* [1980] 1 WLR 17 at 23E-24G and 27E, where a condition precedent that the tenant offer to surrender the tenancy to the landlord before alienation was upheld.

175 Specified in s19(4) as (i) leases of agricultural holdings within the meaning of the Agricultural Holdings Act 1986 and to which that Act applies and (ii) farm business tenancies within the meaning of the Agricultural Tenancies Act 1995.

without the landlord's consent, s19(1)(b) implies a proviso into the covenant that no consent is required to an assignment, underlease or parting with possession made more than seven years before the end of the term, provided that written notice is given to the landlord within six months after the transaction is effected. Again, this proviso applies notwithstanding any express provision to the contrary.

104. However, s19(1)(b) does not apply where:

a) The lessor is a Government department, local or public authority, or a statutory or public utility company[176]; and/or

b) The lease is a mining lease[177] or is a lease of an agricultural holding or a farm business tenancy[178]; and/or

c) The lease is a 'qualifying lease', defined by s19(1E) as *any lease which is a new tenancy for the purposes of section 1 of the Landlord and Tenant (Covenants) Act 1995 other than a residential lease...*" The disapplication of s19(1)(b) to qualifying leases has deprived s19(1)(b) of much practical effect.

---

[176] Section 19(1)(b). For definitions of 'statutory company' and 'public utility company' see s25(1).

[177] Section 19(4). A mining lease is, by s25(1), *"a lease for any mining purpose or purposes connected therewith"*. 'Mining purposes' are defined to *"include the sinking and searching for, winning, working, getting, making merchantable, smelting or otherwise converting or working for the purposes of any manufacture, carrying away, and disposing of mines and minerals, in or under land, and the erection of buildings, and the execution of engineering and other works suitable for those purposes"*.

[178] Section 19(4). Specified in s19(4) as (1) leases of agricultural holdings within the meaning of the Agricultural Holdings Act 1986 and to which that Act applies and (2) to farm business tenancies within the meaning of the Agricultural Tenancies Act 1995.

Landlord and Tenant Act 1988: duty to give consent to applications except where reasonable not to, duty to decide applications within a reasonable time, duty to give reasons for refusing consent, duty to pass on applications

105. The 1988 Act introduced a set of statutory duties intended to ensure that tenant applications for consent are dealt with expeditiously, passed to the correct persons and decided on a reasoned basis.

106. The Act applies in any case where a tenancy contains a covenant against one or more of assigning, underletting, charging or parting with possession of the demised premises, or any part of them, without the consent of the landlord or some other person where the covenant is subject to the qualification that such consent is not to be unreasonably withheld.[179]

107. It follows from the drafting of s1(1) that the Act does not apply to absolute covenants, nor to covenants qualified covenants which do not contain the requirement for landlord consent, such consent not to be unreasonably withheld. It has been held, for example, that the duties imposed by s1 of the Act do not apply to a covenant not to underlet at a rent less than the *"full rack rental value"* of premises[180], but do apply to an obligation not to underlet at a rent less than the passing rent without the consent of the landlord, such consent not to be unreasonably withheld.[181]

108. Where the act applies, a landlord served with a written application for consent to a proposed transaction is under a statutory duty to, within a reasonable time:

---

179 LTA 1988 s1(1).

180 See *Clinton Cards (Essex) Ltd v Sun Alliance and London Assurance Company Ltd* [2002] EWHC 1576; [2003] L & TR 2 at paragraph 21.

181 *Clinton Cards (Essex) Ltd v Sun Alliance and London Assurance Company Ltd* at paragraph 22.

a) Give consent to the transaction except in a case where it is reasonable not to give consent (s1(3)(a)); and

b) Serve on the tenant a written notice of its decision whether or not to give consent. If consent is given, any conditions to which the consent is subject must be specified. If consent is refused, the reasons for withholding it must be given (s1(3)(b)).

109. The s1(3)(a) duty is not satisfied by giving consent subject to a condition which is itself unreasonable (s1(4)).

110. By s1(6), where any one of the s1(3) duties apply, the burden of proof is on the landlord to show that:

a) If consent was given, it was given within a reasonable time;

b) If consent was given subject to a condition, that the condition was reasonable;

c) If consent was refused, that the refusal was reasonable;

d) That the notice of the landlord's decision required by s1(3) was served on the tenant within a reasonable time.

111. It should be noted that s1(6) of the 1988 Act reverses the burden of proof which applies at common law, where it has been held that the onus of proving that consent has been unreasonably withheld is on the tenant.[182]

[182] See *International Drilling Fluids Ltd v Louisville Investments (Uxbridge) Ltd* [1986] Ch 513 at 520. The shifting of the burden of proof onto the landlord by s1 of the 1988 Act was noted by the Court of Appeal in *Kened Ltd v Connie Investments Limited* (1995) 70 P & CR 370 at 374.

112. The Court of Appeal has considered the duties imposed by the Landlord and Tenant 1988 Act on several occasions[183]. The principles derived from those cases are discussed in chapter 6.

113. Similar duties are imposed on a head landlord whose consent is required to a proposed disposition by a sub-tenant.[184] The statutory duties are owed directly to the sub-tenant.[185]

114. The 1988 Act also imposes a statutory duty on recipients of applications for consent to, within a reasonable time, pass them onto other persons who they believe may need to consent to the transaction[186].

115. By s4 of the 1988 Act, a "*claim that a person has broken any duty under this Act may be made the subject of civil proceedings in like manner as any other claim in tort for breach of statutory duty.*" Such claims are considered further in chapter 8.

116. The duties imposed by the 1988 Act bind the Crown[187].

Landlord and Tenant (Covenants) Act 1995 sections 22 and 25 / Landlord and Tenant Act 1927 sections 19(1A) to 19(1E): ability of parties to agree in advance what will amount to a reasonable basis for refusing consent to an assignment

117. Section 22 of the 1995 Act inserted subsections 19(1A) to 19(1E) into s19 of the Landlord and Tenant Act 1927. Prior to those

---

[183] See *Kened Ltd v Connie Investments Limited* (1995) 70 P & CR 370; *Dong Bang Minerva (UK) Ltd v Davina Ltd* (1997) 73 P & CR 253; *Go West Ltd v Spigarolo* [2003] EWCA Civ 17; [2003] QB 1140; *No 1 West India Quay (Residential) Ltd v East Tower Apartments Ltd* [2018] EWCA Civ 250; [2018] 1 WLR 5682.

[184] See s3.

[185] Section 3(2).

[186] See s2(1).

[187] LTA 1988 s6.

amendments, the courts had held that parties could not agree in advance what would be a reasonable basis for withholding consent to an assignment. It was explained in *Bocardo v S&M Hotels*[188] that:

> *"...as a result of section 19(1) the parties cannot by the terms of their contract abrogate the right and duty of the court, in the event of a dispute as to the reasonableness of the withholding of consent where consent is required by the terms of the lease, to decide by all objective standard whether or not the refusal is reasonable. Thus, if the parties by their contract purport to say that in such and such circumstances the landlord may withhold his consent, that term of the contract is invalid and is to be disregarded. The court itself decides whether in the circumstances which actually exist the refusal of consent is reasonable."*

118. The amendments made by the 1995 Act apply to 'qualifying leases' as defined by s19(1E)(a), namely *"any lease which is a new tenancy for the purposes of section 1 of the Landlord and Tenant (Covenants) Act 1995 other than a residential lease..."* Tenancies granted from 1 January 1996 onwards are 'new tenancies' under the 1995 Act.[189]

119. For leases to which the amendments apply, s19(1A) provides that where the landlord and tenant

> *"...have entered into an agreement specifying for the purposes of this subsection—*
>
> > *(a) any circumstances in which the landlord may withhold his licence or consent to an assignment of the demised premises or any part of them, or*
> >
> > *(b) any conditions subject to which any such licence or consent may be granted,*

[188] [1980] 1 WLR 17 at 22E-G.

[189] Section 1(3) LTCA 1995.

then the landlord—

> *(i) shall not be regarded as unreasonably withholding his licence or consent to any such assignment if he withholds it on the ground (and it is the case) that any such circumstances exist, and*
>
> *(ii) if he gives any such licence or consent subject to any such conditions, shall not be regarded as giving it subject to unreasonable conditions;*

and section 1 of the Landlord and Tenant Act 1988 (qualified duty to consent to assignment etc.) shall have effect subject to the provisions of this subsection."

120. It should be noted that:

a) Section 19(1A) is limited to agreements regarding applications for assignment. It does not apply to agreements as to the conditions on which applications to charge premises or sublet them will be withheld[190];

b) By s19(1B), agreements under s19(1A) will include:

   i. Both an agreement contained within the lease itself and an agreement made outside of the lease;

   ii. Agreements made at any time falling before the application for the landlord's consent, not just agreements made on and before the date the lease is granted.

c) Section 19(1C) disapplies s19(1A) to any agreement "*... to the extent that any circumstances or conditions specified in it are framed by reference to any matter falling to be determined by the*

---

190 Section 19(1E)(b) provides that, in s19(1A), *"references to assignment include parting with possession on assignment."*

landlord or by any other person for the purposes of the agreement", unless under the terms of the agreement:

i. That person's power to determine that matter is required to be exercised reasonably; or

ii. The tenant is given an unrestricted right to have any such determination reviewed by a person independent of both landlord and tenant, whose identity is ascertainable by reference to the agreement, and whose determination is provided to be *"conclusive as to the matter in question"*.

121. By s25 of the 1995 Act, any agreement relating to a tenancy is void to the extent that *"it would apart from this section have effect to exclude, modify or otherwise frustrate the operation"* of s22, which inserted subsections 19(1A) to 19(1E) into the LTA 1927. Accordingly, an agreement seeking to exclude, modify or otherwise frustrate the operation of those subsections is void.

Equality Act 2010: prohibition on discriminating against another person by not giving permission for premises to be disposed to that other person

122. By s34(1) of the Equality Act 2010, a *"person whose permission is required for the disposal of premises must not discriminate against another by not giving permission for the disposal of the premises to the other."* For these purposes, a reference to 'premises' includes all or any part of them[191] and a 'disposal' includes, in the case of premises subject to a tenancy, assigning, subletting or parting with the possession of premises[192]. The prohibited discrimination must

[191] Equality Act 2010 s38(2).

[192] Equality Act 2010 s38(3).

relate to one of the protected characteristics specified in s4[193], other than age, marriage and civil partnership to which that Part of the 2010 Act does not apply[194]. Some exceptions are made for owner-occupies and certain small premises.[195]

Partially qualified covenants: restrictions on the landlord's contractual discretion to refuse to give consent

123. This issue rarely arises for alienation covenants as s19(1)(a) of the Landlord and Tenant Act 1927 and s1(3) of the Landlord and Tenant Act 1988 upgrade partially qualified alienation covenants into fully qualified covenants. The court's approach to assessing whether consent under a partially qualified covenant has been unlawfully withheld is discussed in chapter 6.

Fully qualified covenants: the reasonableness test

124. The approach of the courts when assessing whether a landlord has reasonably withheld consent to a proposed transaction under a fully qualified covenant is discussed in detail in chapter 6.

Consequences of the landlord failing to act reasonably in withholding consent

125. Where a tenant considers that their landlord has unreasonably refused consent to a transaction, their options include:

---

[193] Specifically, age; disability; gender reassignment; marriage and civil partnership; pregnancy and maternity; race; religion or belief; sex; sexual orientation.

[194] Equality Act 2010 s32(1).

[195] See s38(9) and Schedule 5 of the Equality Act 2010.

a) Seeking a declaration from the court that consent has been unreasonably withheld[196]; or

b) Proceeding with the transaction without consent. If the tenant is correct that consent has been unreasonably withheld, to do so will not be a breach of the lease[197]; or

c) Claiming damages from the landlord for the breach of the statutory duties imposed by the 1988 Act.

126. These possibilities, and the underlying case law, are discussed in detail in chapter 8. Seeking a declaration from the court, prior to entering into the transaction, is ordinarily the safer if slower option.

Liability of tenants following an assignment: Landlord and Tenant (Covenants) Act 1995

Assignor's and assignee's future liability under the tenant covenants following an assignment

127. Prior to the amendments to the law made by the Landlord and Tenant (Covenants) Act 1995 ("LTCA 1995"), the original landlord to a lease could enforce the tenant covenants against the original tenant throughout the term due to the privity of contract between them. This was the case even if the original tenant had assigned the lease to another and it was the assignee who then breached the covenant, not the original tenant.[198] One of the

---

[196] The County Court has jurisdiction to hear such a claim: s53 of the Landlord and Tenant Act 1954.

[197] *Treloar v Bigge* (1874) LR 9 Ex 151. This case and the line of case law which follows it is considered in chapter 8.

[198] See, for example, *Hill v East and West India Dock Co* (1884) 9 App Cas 448 at 453. In contrast, an assignee tenant (B) would not be liable for breaches of covenant committed by a successor assignee (C). This is because B's liability is dependent upon privity of estate with the landlord, which ceases as soon as the privity of estate is destroyed by the assignment to C: see *Paul v Nurse* (1828) 8 Barnewall and Cresswell 486, where the Court explained

purposes of the LTCA 1995 was, for 'new tenancies', to abolish this onerous rule.

128. Tenancies granted from 1 January 1996 onwards are 'new tenancies' and are government by the LTCA 1995[199].

129. Section 3(1) of the Act provides for the transmission of the benefit and burden of the covenants in a tenancy, providing that:

"(1) The benefit and burden of all landlord and tenant covenants of a tenancy—

(a) shall be annexed and incident to the whole, and to each and every part, of the premises demised by the tenancy and of the reversion in them, and

(b) shall in accordance with this section pass on an assignment of the whole or any part of those premises or of the reversion in them."

130. Section 3(2) continues that:

"(2) Where the assignment is by the tenant under the tenancy, then as from the assignment the assignee—

(a) becomes bound by the tenant covenants of the tenancy except to the extent that—

(i) immediately before the assignment they did not bind the assignor, or

---

that the action in that case was: "... *founded on privity of estate*" and that "*the obligation of the defendants to perform the covenant arose only from their filling the particular character of assignees of the estate, which the lessee had under the lease. As soon, therefore, as they ceased to be assignees, their obligation to perform the covenant was at an end.*"

[199] Section 1(3) Landlord and Tenant (Covenants) Act 1995 and the Landlord and Tenant (Covenants) Act 1995 (Commencement) Order 1995 (SI 1995/2963).

(ii) they fall to be complied with in relation to any demised premises not comprised in the assignment; and

(b) becomes entitled to the benefit of the landlord covenants of the tenancy except to the extent that they fall to be complied with in relation to any such premises."

131. By these provisions, the assignee tenant is from the date of the assignment:

a) Entitled to the benefit of the landlord covenants; but

b) Is subject to the burden of the tenant covenants.

132. Section 28(1) defines:

a) 'Landlord' and 'tenant' respectively as *"the person for the time being entitled to the reversion expectant on the term of the tenancy and the person so entitled to that term"*;

b) 'Tenancy' as *"any lease or other tenancy"*, including a sub-tenancy or agreement for a tenancy, but not a mortgage term;

c) 'Covenant' as including any *"term, condition and obligation"* and references to a covenant of a tenancy *"include a covenant...contained in a collateral agreement"*;

d) 'Tenant covenant' as, in relation to a tenancy, *"a covenant falling to be complied with by the tenant of premises demised by the tenancy"*;

e) 'Assignment' as including an *"equitable assignment"* and, subject to s11, including an *"assignment in breach of a covenant of a tenancy or by operation of law"*.

133. Section 5(1)-(3) provides for the release of the assignor tenant upon the assignment, changing the position from the previously applicable law:

"(1) This section applies where a tenant assigns premises demised to him under a tenancy.

(2) If the tenant assigns the whole of the premises demised to him, he—

(a) is released from the tenant covenants of the tenancy, and

(b) ceases to be entitled to the benefit of the landlord covenants of the tenancy,

as from the assignment.

(3) If the tenant assigns part only of the premises demised to him, then as from the assignment he—

(a) is released from the tenant covenants of the tenancy, and

(b) ceases to be entitled to the benefit of the landlord covenants of the tenancy;

only to the extent that those covenants fall to be complied with in relation to that part of the demised premises…"

134. By these provisions, the assignor tenant is from the date of the assignment:

   a) No longer entitled to the benefit of the landlord covenants; but

   b) Is not subject to the burden of the tenant covenants in the future.

Assignor's and assignee's rights and liabilities for past breaches of covenant

135. At common law, an assignor tenant remained liable for any breaches of covenant committed prior to the assignment. Section 24(1) of the LTCA 1995 preserves this rule, stating that: *"Any release of a*

person from a covenant by virtue of this Act does not affect any liability of his arising from a breach of the covenant occurring before the release."

136. Likewise, at common law, an assignor tenant remained able to claim in respect of landlord breaches of covenant committed prior to the assignment. Section 24(4) of the LTCA 1995 preserves that rule, stating that: *"Where by virtue of this Act a person ceases to be entitled to the benefit of a covenant, this does not affect any rights of his arising from a breach of the covenant occurring before he ceases to be so entitled."*

137. The assignor tenant's rights in respect of past breaches of landlord covenants may, however, be assigned to the assignee tenant.[200]

138. At common law, an assignee tenant was not liable for any breaches of the tenant covenants committed prior to the assignment.[201] Nor was the assignee tenant able to claim in respect of past breaches of the landlord covenants which pre-date the assignment.[202]

139. Section 23(1) of the LTCA 1995 preserves both rules, stating that:

"Where as a result of an assignment a person becomes, by virtue of this Act, bound by or entitled to the benefit of a covenant, he shall not by virtue of this Act have any liability or rights under the covenant in relation to any time falling before the assignment."

140. However, s23(2) provides that *"subsection (1) does not preclude any such rights being expressly assigned to the person in question."* The assignor tenant may, therefore, assign their rights in respect of past breaches of landlord covenants to the assignee tenant.

---

200 Section 23(2).

201 The assignee would, however, become liable under the covenants if the breach was a continuing one, such as a failure to keep the premises in repair.

202 Again, the assignee would be able to claim in respect of continuing breaches of the landlord covenants.

Excluded assignments

141. The provisions of s5 of the LTCA 1995 which automatically release an assigning tenant (A) from liability under the tenant covenants do not apply where the assignment is 'excluded'[203]. Instead, those provisions have effect *"as from the next assignment (if any) of the premises assigned by [A] which is not an excluded assignment."*[204]

142. An 'excluded assignment' is an assignment *"in breach of a covenant of a tenancy or... by operation of law"*[205].

143. The effect of s11 is that, where a tenant (A) assigns in breach of covenant to B, and B then assigns with the landlord's consent to C:

    a) For the duration of B's tenure, A remains liable under the tenant covenants but also may enforce the landlord covenants;

    b) Upon the assignment to C, A is released from the tenant covenants and loses the right to enforce the landlord covenants.

Authorised guarantee agreements

144. Section 16(1) of the LTCA 1995 provides that nothing in the Act[206] precludes a landlord on an assignment by the tenant which releases it from a tenant covenant by virtue of the Act from *"entering into an authorised guarantee agreement with respect to the performance of that covenant by the assignee"*. Agreements which are not 'authorised guarantee agreements' and which seek to restrict the

[203] Section 11(2)(a).

[204] Section 11(2)(b).

[205] Section 11(1).

[206] In particular the anti-avoidance provisions in s25.

operation of the LTCA 1995 are likely to be void by virtue of the anti-avoidance provisions in s25.

145. An agreement is an 'authorised guarantee agreement' if:

a) Under the agreement the tenant guarantees the performance of the relevant covenant to any extent by the assignee; and

b) It is entered into in the circumstances set out in s16(3); and

c) Its provisions conform with s16(4) and s16(5).[207]

146. The circumstances specified by s16(3) are that:

a) By virtue of a covenant against assignment (whether absolute or qualified) the assignment cannot be effected without the consent of the landlord under the tenancy or some other person[208]; and

b) Any such consent is given subject to a condition (lawfully imposed) that the tenant is to enter into an agreement guaranteeing the performance of the covenant by the assignee[209]; and

c) The agreement is entered into by the tenant in pursuance of that condition[210].

147. Section 16(4) provides that an agreement is not an authorised guarantee agreement *"to the extent that it purports"*:

[207] Section 16(2).

[208] Section 16(3)(a).

[209] Section 16(3)(b).

[210] Section 16(3)(c).

a) To impose on the tenant any requirement to guarantee in any way the performance of the relevant covenant by any person other than the assignee[211]; or

b) To impose on the tenant any liability, restriction or other requirement (of whatever nature) in relation to any time after the assignee is released from that covenant by virtue of the Act[212].

148. By s16(5), subject to s16(4), an authorised guarantee agreement may:

a) Impose on the tenant any liability as sole or principal debtor in respect of any obligation owed by the assignee under the relevant covenant;

b) Impose on the tenant liabilities as guarantor in respect of the assignee's performance of that covenant which are no more onerous than those to which he would be subject in the event of his being liable as sole or principal debtor in respect of any obligation owed by the assignee under that covenant;

c) Require the tenant, in the event of the tenancy assigned by him being disclaimed, to enter into a new tenancy of the premises comprised in the assignment[213].

149. By these provisions, where there is a covenant against assignment in a lease and the landlord lawfully makes it a condition of a proposed assignment that the tenant enter into an authorised guarantee agreement and the tenant does so, the assignor tenant will

---

[211] Section 16(4)(a).

[212] Section 16(4)(b).

[213] Provided its term *"expires not later than the term of the tenancy assigned by the tenant"* and whose *"tenant covenants are no more onerous than those of that tenancy"*.

(as guarantor) remain liable under the tenant covenants until such time as their successor assigns the lease on to another tenant.[214]

When may a landlord require a tenant to enter into an authorised guarantee agreement?

150. A landlord may require a tenant to enter into an authorised guarantee agreement as a condition of consenting to an assignment where:

a) There is an absolute covenant against alienation; or

b) For tenancies containing a qualified covenant against alienation, where:

i. The tenancy provides that entry into an authorised guarantee agreement will be a condition of the landlord giving consent to an assignment (in accordance with s19(1A) of the Landlord and Tenant Act 1927[215]); or

ii. Where it is reasonable to require the tenant to enter into such an agreement. An unreasonable attempt to impose such a condition would fall foul of s1 of the Landlord and Tenant Act 1988, and so not be 'lawfully imposed' under s16(3)(b) of the LTCA 1995.

151. In practice, most commercial tenancies contain an express provision that entry into an authorised guarantee agreement will be a condition of the landlord consenting to an assignment of the tenancy.

---

[214] Any attempt to make the assignor tenant remain liable for further assignments will go beyond the terms permitted by s16(4)(a).

[215] Discussed above.

Liability of assignees under direct covenants

152. At common law, an assignee tenant (B) was not liable for breaches of covenant committed by a successor assignee (C). This is because B's liability was dependent upon privity of estate with the landlord, which ceased as soon as the privity of estate was destroyed by the assignment to C.[216] Liability could be imposed, however, by B covenanting directly with the landlord to perform the tenant covenants for the duration of the term, creating privity of contract between them.[217]

153. In the absence of such a direct covenant, B's release from the tenant covenants derives from the common law, not from the LTCA 1995. This matters because s16(1) permits authorised guarantee agreements where a tenant is released from a tenant covenant *"by virtue of this Act"*, but not otherwise. In such a situation, B cannot be required to enter into an authorised guarantee agreement, even if the landlord's consent is required for the onward assignment.

154. In practice, assignee tenants are usually required, as a condition of the landlord's consent, to enter into a direct covenant with the landlord to perform the tenant covenants for the duration of the term[218]. The assignee tenant's release upon a further assignment is

---

216 See *Paul v Nurse* (1828) 8 Barnewall and Cresswell 486, where the Court explained that the action in that case was: *"... founded on privity of estate"* and that *"the obligation of the defendants to perform the covenant arose only from their filling the particular character of assignees of the estate, which the lessee had under the lease. As soon, therefore, as they ceased to be assignees, their obligation to perform the covenant was at an end."*

217 Achieved by the lessor requiring an incoming assignee (B) to enter into such a covenant as one of the conditions on which consent to assign is given to the existing tenant (A). For an example where an assignee was held liable under such a direct covenant, see *J Lyons & Co Ltd v Knowles* [1943] 1 KB 366.

218 Although the covenant is contained within the licence to assign, this is a tenant covenant within the meaning of s28(1) which defines 'covenant' as including a covenant *"contained in a collateral agreement"*.

then achieved by virtue of the Act, thereby enabling the landlord to require B to enter into an authorised guarantee agreement.

Excluded assignments and authorised guarantee agreements

155. As discussed above, on an excluded assignment the assigning tenant (A) remains liable under the tenant covenants and so the issue of entering into an authorised guarantee agreement does not arise[219]. However, on a further assignment by the then tenant (B), A would be released from further liability. If the tenancy contains an absolute or qualified covenant against alienation, the landlord may be able to require both A and B to enter into authorised guarantee agreements as guarantors of the new tenant's (C's) performance of the tenant covenants. This may be appropriate where, for example, B is a company with few assets such that (1) the landlord would not have consented to the assignment to B in the first place; and (2) the value to the landlord of B as a guarantor is minimal.

Position of guarantors

156. Section 24(2) of the LTCA 1995 provides that, where a tenant is released from a tenant covenant of a tenancy, any other person who immediately before the release was *"bound by a covenant of the tenancy imposing any liability or penalty in the event of a failure to comply with that tenant covenant"* is released from that obligation *"to the same extent as the tenant is release from that tenant covenant"*. The effect of s24(2) is that, where a tenant is released from liability under the Act, so too is any person who guaranteed their performance of that obligation. An attempt to make a guarantor guarantee the performance of not only the tenant (A), but their

[219] Further, s16(1) makes provision for authorised guarantee agreements where *"on an assignment a tenant is to any extent released from a tenant covenant of a tenancy by virtue of this Act"* – as explained above that does not occur on an excluded assignment.

assigns as well, will be void under the anti-avoidance provisions of the Act.[220]

157. The Court of Appeal has, however, held that it is permissible under the LTCA 1995 for a assigning tenant's (A's) guarantor to guarantee A's performance under an authorised guarantee agreement.[221]

Attempts to exclude the operation of the LTCA 1995

158. Section 25 of the LTCA 1995 contains strong anti-avoidance provisions, by which any agreement relating to tenancy is void to the extent that:

a) It would *"apart from this section have effect to exclude, modify or otherwise frustrate the operation of any provision of this Act"*[222];

b) It provides for (i) the termination or surrender of the tenancy or (ii) the imposition on the tenant of any penalty, disability or liability in the event of, in connection with or in consequence of the operation of the provisions of the Act[223].

159. Section 25(3) confirms that *"nothing in this section applies to any agreement to the extent that it is an authorised guarantee agreement"*.

---

[220] See *K/S Victoria Street v House of Fraser (Stores Management) Ltd* [2011] EWCA Civ 904; [2012] Ch 497 at paragraph 21.

[221] *K/S Victoria Street v House of Fraser (Stores Management) Ltd* [2011] EWCA Civ 904; [2012] Ch 497 at paragraph 46.

[222] Section 25(1)(a).

[223] Sections 25(1)(b)-(c).

Summary

160. The essential points can be summarised as follows:

a) Leases are alienable property – as a matter of principle, unless restricted by the lease, a tenant may without the need for consent assign their interest to somebody else or underlet or share possession or occupation or the premises;

b) Even if the lease prohibits alienation, that will not of itself invalidate an assignment or sub-lease;

c) Because the unauthorised assignment is effective to vest the remainder of the term in the assignee, the correct recipient of a s146 notice is the assignee, not the assigning tenant;

d) There is a long line of case law which supports interpreting alienation covenants strictly, giving effect to the technical distinctions between legal and equitable interests and between assigning, sub-letting, sharing possession and sharing occupation and between (1) restrictions which apply to the whole of premises only and (2) restrictions which apply to all or part;

e) Despite the modern approach to interpretation being more flexible than was the case when many those cases were decided, these distinctions are likely to continue to be given effect by the courts when interpreting alienation clauses because (1) such clauses cut down the lessee's rights and (2) the consequence of breaching the covenant is forfeiture;

f) Qualified alienation covenants have been the subject of significant statutory interventions, including:

   i. A prohibition on taking fines as a condition of consent (s144 Law of Property Act 1925);

ii. A duty not to unreasonably withhold consent (s19(1)(a) Landlord and Tenant Act 1927);

iii. Duties imposed by the Landlord and Tenant Act 1988 to:

    1. Give consent to the transaction within a reasonable time except in a case where it is reasonable not to give consent (s1(3)(a)); and

    2. Within a reasonable time, to serve on the tenant a written notice of its decision whether or not to give consent. Where consent is withheld, the burden of proving that the refusal was reasonable is upon the landlord, which a reversal of the common law position;

g) The parties may agree in advance what will be a reasonable basis for withholding consent to an assignment (ss19(1A) to 19(1E) LTA 1927).

CHAPTER FOUR

RULES GOVERNING ALTERATION COVENANTS

Tenants' rights to alter premises

161. At common law, a tenant has the right to alter the demised premises as an incident of their rights of ownership[224]. That right is, however, subject to:

   a) The tenant covenants in the lease, both express and implied; and

   b) The obligation in tort not to commit voluntary waste.

Voluntary waste

162. The law of waste is of ancient origin and is both highly complicated and deeply uncertain. For detailed consideration, reference should be made to specialist works and/or to the helpful report of the Law Commission where the nature of waste and its complexities were considered.[225] The Law Commission recommended its abolition[226] but those recommendations were not acted upon.

163. There are two forms of waste: (1) voluntary waste, which relates to positive acts which harm the landlord's reversion and (2) permissive

---

[224] As noted by Buckley J in *West Ham Central Charity Board v East London Waterworks Company* [1900] 1 Ch 624 at 636, within the covenants imposed by the lease and the obligations imposed in tort not to commit a voluntary waste, the tenant *"may use his holding as he pleases"*.

[225] (1996) Law Com. No.238 Pt X.

[226] Subject to narrow exceptions.

waste, which relates to a failure to take steps to prevent damage to property from an outside cause.

164. It is unlikely that permissive waste will be relevant in the current context and the discussion below is limited to voluntary waste. There are significant uncertainties about when, if at all, permissive waste applies to tenants and what it actually requires.[227]

Which occupiers are subject to the obligation not to commit voluntary waste?

165. Tenants under a term of years (i.e. fixed term tenants) are under a duty in tort not to commit voluntary waste.[228] The courts have also found that periodic tenants are under a duty in tort not to commit a voluntary waste.[229]

166. Where a tenant at will commits a voluntary waste, that has the effect of automatically terminating the tenancy and the landlord may bring an action in trespass.[230] Where a tenant at sufferance commits a voluntary waste, the landlord may elect to treat him as a trespasser, or waive the trespass and bring an action in the tort of waste.[231] However, the correctness of the case law establishing these rules has

---

[227] See the discussion of the Law Commission at (1996) Law Com. No.238 Pt X. paragraphs 10.19 to 10.25.

[228] As to the duty being tortious rather than contractual, see *Defries v Milne* [1913] 1 Ch 98 at 108. The origin of the duty is the Statute of Marlborough 1267. The ancient statutes were analysed in detail by the court in *Dayani v London Borough of Bromley* (No 1) [1999] 3 EGLR 144.

[229] See, for tenancies for year to year, *Marsden v Edward Heyes Ltd* [1927] 2 KB 1. It is tolerably clear in this case that the court considered that both tortious and contractual duties applied – see the comments of Bankes LJ at 4 and 5-6 and of Atkin LJ at 8. For weekly tenancies, see *Warren v Keen* [1954] 1 QB 15, although this case is less clear as to whether the obligation under discussion is tortious or contractual.

[230] *Countess of Shrewsbury's Case* (1600) 5 CO Rep 13b; 77 ER 68.

[231] *Burchell v HornsbyI* 170 ER 795; (1808) 1 Camp. 360.

been doubted.[232] These issues are unlikely to arise in the context of tenant alterations.

167. It is uncertain whether a licensee can commit waste. The author is aware of no clear authority on the point.

What is voluntary waste?

168. Voluntary waste is the deliberate or negligent[233] commission of an act which damages the demised premises, to the injury of the landlord's reversion[234]. Case law confirms that:

   a) Damage to landlord's reversion is an essential component of the tort. In *Doe d. Grubb v Burlington*[235], Denman CJ held the principle to be that *"where there are no damages there can be no waste"* and that:

      "...there is no authority for saying that any act can be waste which is not injurious to the inheritance, either, first, by diminishing the value of the estate, or, secondly, by increasing the [burden] upon it, or, thirdly, by impairing the evidence of title."[236]

   b) Similarly, an act which causes only de minimis harm to the landlord's reversion will not amount to waste: *"if the value be very small, the consequences of waste do not attach"*[237];

---

[232] See the report of the Law Commission (1996) Law Com. No.238 Pt X at paragraphs 10.23 and 10.24.

[233] On the requirement for the act to be deliberate or negligent, see *Manchester Bonded Warehouse Company Ltd v Carr* (1880) 5 CPD 507 at 512.

[234] See *Mancetter Developments Ltd v Garmanson* [1986] QB 1212 at 1218D-E.

[235] (1833) 5 B & Ad 507.

[236] At 517.

[237] *Doe d. Grubb v Burlington* (1833) 5 B & Ad 507 at 516.

c) The tort is (almost invariably) applicable only to positive acts, not omissions[238];

d) Acts of the tenant which cause damage to the demised premises but are neither deliberate nor negligent will not amount to a voluntary waste. Absent provision in the lease to the contrary, a tenant is *"...not liable for the destruction of the property let to him if such destruction is in fact due to nothing more than a reasonable use of the property"*, where that use is *"for a purpose for which the property was intended to be used"* and the mode and extent of the user was proper having regard to (1) the nature of the property; (2) what the tenant knew of it and (3) what as an ordinary business man he ought to have known of it. To do otherwise would be to hold a tenant liable for latent faults and defects in the property demised.[239] The parties may, however, impose liability on the tenant in such circumstances by express agreement.[240]

169. A wide range of acts can potentially amount to a waste. Essentially, a waste can include any act which damages the demised premises so as to cause damage to the reversion. Examples from the case law of acts which could potentially amount to a waste[241] include the destruction of the building in which the demised premises were located[242] by overloading a floor, pulling down an outbuilding

---

238 See *Mancetter Developments Ltd v Garmanson* [1986] QB 1212 at 1222D-E and 1224G. Kerr LJ was of the view that *"an omission to do something can hardly ever, and perhaps never, constitute an act of voluntary waste"*.

239 *Manchester Bonded Warehouse Company Ltd v Carr* (1880) 5 CPD 507 at 512.

240 *Manchester Bonded Warehouse Company Ltd v Carr* (1880) 5 CPD 507 at 512.

241 Dependent on a deliberate or negligent act and on there being damage to the reversion.

242 *Manchester Bonded Warehouse Company Ltd v Carr* (1880) 5 CPD 507.

within the demised premises[243] and the breaking of windows or doors[244].

170. As for the installation and the removal of fixtures:

a) The removal of the landlord's fixtures will amount to a waste[245];

b) The removal of tenant fixtures without making good the resulting damage caused to the structure of the demised premises will amount to a waste[246];

c) The case law is less clear as to whether it is a waste to damage the demised premises when installing tenant fixtures. The issue split the Court of Appeal in *Mancetter Developments Ltd v Garmanson*[247]. In that case, a tenant cut holes in the outside walls of industrial premises in order to install pipes and extractor fans. Five years later, a successor occupier removed the pipes and fans but did not fill the holes. Sir George Waller considered that the waste occurred when the holes were first

---

243 Provided damage to the reversion results – see, in the context of pulling down a barn outbuilding, *Doe d. Grubb v Burlington* (1833) 5 B & Ad 507 at 516.

244 See the judgment of Denning LJ in *Warren v Keen* [1954] 1 QB 15 at 21.

245 See *Mancetter Developments Ltd v Garmanson* [1986] QB 1212 at 1218F-G and 1219H.

246 See *Mancetter Developments Ltd v Garmanson* [1986] QB 1212 at 1219H, where Dillon LJ explained that: *"the liability to make good the damage is a condition of the tenant's right to remove tenant's fixtures; therefore removal of the fixtures without making good the damage, being in excess of the tenant's right of removal, is waste, actionable in tort, just as much as removal by the tenant of a landlord's fixture which the tenant has no right to remove is waste."* Dillon LJ confirmed that the liability attracts to the person who removed the fixtures without making good, not to the person who installed them: 1219G.

247 [1986] QB 1212.

cut[248]. Kerr LJ was of the oppose view, arguing that given the use of the premises for a chemicals business, in installing the pipes and extractor fan the tenant was acting in accordance with its lease and the landlord could not have sued the tenant for waste as soon as the holes had been made.[249] The author's view is that the judgment of Kerr LJ is to be preferred, such that necessary damage caused in the course of installing trade fixtures, where reasonably contemplated by the lease, will not amount to a waste at the time of installation.[250]

171. As above, at common law a tenant may alter the demised premises subject to the controls imposed by the lease and the duty in tort not to commit voluntary waste. Alterations to the demised premises will amount to a voluntary waste where they result in a 'substantial change' in the character of the demised premises.

172. To ascertain whether as a result of tenant alterations there has been a substantial change in the character of premises demised, which is a question of fact[251], it is necessary to examine the terms of the lease[252], in particular the permissible user under the lease[253]. Examples given in the case law of what would amount to a substantial change in character include:

248 See 1222C: *"In the present case there can be little doubt that Pilot, when it made the holes, was guilty of waste. What it had done was a "spoil or destruction" to the building."*

249 See 1224C-D.

250 This view will also avoid potential limitation problems from time running from the installation of the fixtures at the outset of the lease.

251 *Hyman v Rose* [1912] AC 623 at 632.

252 *West Ham Central Charity Board v East London Waterworks Company* [1900] 1 Ch 624 at 636.

253 Hyman *v Rose* [1912] AC 623 at 632.

a) Converting pasture land into plough land[254];

b) Breaking up ancient meadows[255];

c) Converting a dwelling house and ground floor shop into one large shop with a loft, achieved by removing partition walls, fireplaces, a staircase, windows and doors[256].

173. In *Hyman v Rose*[257], the House of Lords held that the conversion of a chapel into a cinema, which involved the removal of iron railings, the opening of a new door and internal alterations did not amount to a waste. The lease did not prohibit the contemplated user or the internal alterations required to enable such a use[258], the iron railing had not been shown to be in existence at the date of the demise and the opening of the door had caused no harm to the reversion[259].

Relationship between the terms of the lease and the duty in tort

174. In *Mancetter Developments Ltd v Garmanson*[260], considering the availability of the tort of waste where a lease makes express provision for the repair and condition of the premises, Kerr LJ suggested, but without expressing any concluded opinion, that in such a case it is doubtful *"...whether there would be much scope for the application of the tort of waste"*, the landlord being *"bound to sue on the reinstatement or repairing covenants, or contractually binding*

[254] *West Ham Central Charity Board v East London Waterworks Company* [1900] 1 Ch 624 at 636

[255] *West Ham Central Charity Board v East London Waterworks Company* [1900] 1 Ch 624 at 636

[256] *Marsden v Edward Heyes Ltd* [1927] 2 KB 1. The Court of Appeal was unanimous that this amounted to a voluntary waste – see page 4.

[257] [1912] AC 623.

[258] See 631.

[259] See 632.

[260] [1986] QB 1212.

conditions vis-a-vis licensees, and not on the basis of the tort of waste".[261]

175. It is considered that the weight of the case law goes the other way, holding that the presence of a repairing/reinstatement covenant does not preclude the application of the tort of waste and the landlord may elect between its contractual and tortious remedies.[262]

176. The practical relevance of this issue, noted by the court in *Mancetter Developments Ltd*, is that through use of the tortious cause of action it would be possible to proceed against the director of a tenant company which committed a waste, which would not be possible under the lease unless the director was a guarantor.

177. It is considered that it is open to the parties to reduce the scope of the tortious duty by the terms of the lease, such that a covenant which is inconsistent with the duty in tort will prevail in the case of conflict. For example, in *Mancetter Developments Ltd v Garmanson* Dillon LJ recognised that just as the common law rights of a tenant to remove its fixtures could be *"confirmed or excluded"* by the contract, so the obligation in the tort of waste to make good damage caused by the removal of tenant fixtures could be modified by the contract.[263]

Implied obligation of tenants to use the premises in a tenant like manner

178. One of the complexities in the law of voluntary waste is that is

---

[261] 1223B and D.

[262] See *Defries v Milne* [1913] 1 Ch 98 at 108; *Marsden v Edward Heyes Ltd* [1927] 2 KB 1 at 7-8 (Atkin LJ); *Mancetter Developments Ltd v Garmanson* [1986] QB 1212 at 1219H-1220A; *Regis Property Co Ltd v Dudley* [1959] AC 370 at 407 (Lord Denning), where the obligation not to commit waste was described as a *"separate and distinct"* obligation from those imposed by a covenant to repair and which gave rise to *"separate and distinct remedies"*.

[263] *Mancetter Developments Ltd v Garmanson* [1986] QB 1212 at 1219E-F.

overlaps substantially with an implied contractual duty upon tenants to use the demised premises in a 'tenant like manner' and yield up the demised premises in a condition consistent with the performance of that duty. As with waste, the scope of the obligation to use premises in a tenant like manner, and when the obligation will be implied, are somewhat uncertain.

179. In *Marsden v Edward Heyes Ltd*, responding to an argument that a tortious claim was time barred because the change in the character of the demised premises occurred more than six years prior, Scrutton LJ found that that argument:

> *"...overlooks their implied obligation as tenants to deliver up the demised premises. In my opinion there is an implied contract by a tenant to use the premises in a tenantlike manner and to deliver them up at the end of the term unless prevented from so doing by the act of God. To use premises in a tenantlike manner means at any rate that a tenant will not make such structural alterations in the premises as will change their character. If a dwelling-house is let and something which is not a dwelling-house is delivered up, the contract to deliver up in a tenantlike condition is broken."*[264]

180. As to the content of the obligation, Lord Denning emphasised in *Regis Property Co Ltd v Dudley*[265] that it is not an obligation of repair. Examples of what is required were given by Lord Denning in his earlier decision in *Warren v Keen*:

> *The tenant must take proper care of the place. He must, if he is going away for the winter, turn off the water and empty the boiler. He must clean the chimneys, when necessary, and also the windows. He must mend the electric light when it fuses. He must unstop the sink when it is blocked by his waste. In short, he must do the little jobs about the place which a reasonable tenant would do. In addition, he must, of course, not damage the house, wilfully or negligently; and he must see*

[264] [1927] 2 KB 1 at 7.

[265] [1959] AC 370 at 407.

that his family and guests do not damage it: and if they do, he must repair it. But apart from such things, if the house falls into disrepair through fair wear and tear or lapse of time, or for any reason not caused by him, then the tenant is not liable to repair it.[266]

Uncertainties with the current law

181. The Law Commission[267] identified several uncertainties in the law as it stands including:

   a) Whether a licensee can be liable for the tort of waste;

   b) Whether a licensee can be under an implied obligation of tenant like user;

   c) The precise interrelationship between the tort of waste and the implied obligation of tenant like user;

   d) The content of the tenant's implied obligation of tenantlike user, including whether the obligation varies according to the form of tenure;

   e) Whether the implied obligation of tenant like user is ousted by an express repairing covenant in the tenancy.

182. In practice, given these ongoing uncertainties and the fact that most commercial leases make detailed provision for the condition of the premises, tortious claims for voluntary waste and claims for breach of the implied obligation of tenant like user are rare.

Tenant covenants in the lease: forms of express alteration covenant

183. In practice, most commercial leases impose detailed controls upon the tenant's ability to alter the premises by an express alterations

---

[266] *Warren v Keen* [1954] 1 QB 15 at 20.

[267] (1996) Law Com. No.238 Pt X. at paragraphs 10.31.

covenant. As with alienation covenants, alteration covenants can be usefully divided into three categories:

a) Absolute covenants – which prohibit any alterations, or a class of alterations, outright;

b) Partially qualified covenants – which prevent alterations, or a class of them, without the consent of the landlord;

c) Fully qualified covenants – which prevent alterations, or a class of them, without the consent of the landlord such consent not to be unreasonably withheld.

184. The workings of such covenants are considered below.

Tenant covenants in the lease: other covenants relevant to alterations

185. Express alterations clauses aside, there are a number of other clauses which can be relevant to alterations. They include:

a) The covenant to comply with statutes. This may be relevant where alterations are made other than in compliance with applicable building and planning regulations;

b) Repairing covenants, as

i. The alterations may damage the demised premises in breach of an obligation to keep them in repair;

ii. If the alterations become part of the demised premises they will become subject to tenant obligations of repair;

c) Reinstatement covenants, for example where the tenant is required to remove tenant alterations at the end of the term.

186. As above, the implied obligation to use the premises in a tenant like manner can also be relevant to alterations.

Repairing covenants and alterations

When will alterations breach a repairing covenant?

187. There is a line of case law in which the courts have interpreted repairing covenants as including, by implication, an obligation not to destroy any part of the demised premises. In *Gange v Lockwood*[268], Willes J directed a jury that a "*...covenant to repair, uphold and maintain, or keep in good repair, raises a duty not to destroy the demised premises; and the pulling them down, wholly or partly, is a breach of such covenant.*" More recently, in *Devonshire Reid Properties Ltd v Trenaman*[269], the court held the principle to be that "*...a covenant to repair and maintain raises a duty not to destroy wholly or partly and a proposal to do so is a breach of such covenant.*"

188. On this approach alterations which necessitate causing some damage to the demised premises as part of their installation, as will usually be the case, will amount to a breach of the repairing covenant.

189. However, insofar as those cases have treated this as an independent rule of law or an automatic implication to be made into every repairing covenant, they have gone too far. The court has subsequently declined to follow *Devonshire Reid Properties Ltd v Trenaman* on this point[270] and in *British Glass Manufacturers Confederation v University of Sheffield*[271], Lewison J explained that the principle "*is not an absolute rule of law*" but rather was a "*conclusion reached as a question of construction of the lease.*"

190. Once it is recognised that it is a question of construction whether a repairing covenant will be breached the tenant destroying any part

---

[268] (1860) 2 *Foster and Finlason* 115.

[269] [1997] 1 EGLR 45 at 46.

[270] See *Hannon v 169 Queen's Gate Ltd* [2000] 1 EGLR 40 at 43.

[271] [2004] L & TR 14.

of the demised premises, it can be seen that not every alteration will necessitate a breach of the repairing covenant. Relevant factors in interpreting the repairing covenant will include:

a) The presence of absence of an alterations covenant and its form. For example, if only structural alterations are controlled, that is an indication that the lease envisages that non-structural alterations may be undertaken without breaching the covenants[272];

b) The users permitted by the lease. In *Hyman v Rose*[273], Earl Loreburn LC held that, in the case of a chapel converted into a cinema, that as regards *"internal changes relating to the staircase and the level of the floor"*, they were *"quite legitimate"* for the cinema use permitted by the lease, that being *"the governing consideration"*.[274]

Alterations become part of the demised premises and so subject to any obligation of repair

191. It is a general rule of the common law that anything which is attached to land becomes part of it. The case law sometimes refers to this rule by the Latin maxim 'quicquid plantatur solo, solo cedit' - whatever is affixed to the soil belongs to the soil.

192. Its application in the leasehold context is that, where land is subject to a lease, things attached to the demised premises (i.e. alterations,

[272] See the dissenting judgment of Buckley LJ in *Rose v Spicer* [1911] 2 KB 234, in particular 255, with which the House of Lords subsequently agreed in *Hyman v Rose* [1912] A.C. 623. In that case, the House of Lords held that a covenant not to vary the front elevation, and a covenant for supporting, upholding, and maintaining the premises, was not to be regarded as a covenant prohibiting the internal alterations made, such as the removal of staircases and raising the floor levels – 631-632.

[273] [1912] A.C. 623.

[274] 632.

additions) become part of them and references in a lease to the 'demised premises' will ordinarily be taken to include them.

193. This rule has been recognised on a number of occasions. For example:

a) In *Never-Stop Railway (Wembley) Ltd v British Empire Exhibition (1924) Inc*[275], Lawrence J considered it *"well settled that, in the absence of an agreement to the contrary, any building erected by the tenant upon the demised land immediately becomes part of the land itself"*;

b) In *Ponsford v HMS Aerosols Ltd*[276], Lord Fraser explained that:

"There is no dispute that 'the demised premises,' which originally meant the factory described in clause 1 of the lease now means the factory as rebuilt after the fire, including the improvements made at the expense of the tenants, with the approval of the landlord... The premises would have included the improvements without express provision to that effect, on the principle that anything made part of the premises by the tenants enures to the landlord"

c) In *Peel Land & Property (Port No.3) Ltd v TS Sheerness Steel Ltd*[277], Rimer LJ stated that:

"Since a new building becomes part of the land upon which it is built, and therefore must become part of "the site" upon which it is built, there is, so it seems to me, a logical argument for the proposition that "the said premises" ought to be interpreted in an "always speaking" sense, and therefore as including new

275 [1926] Ch 877 at 885.

276 [1979] AC 63 at 83-83.

277 [2014] EWCA Civ 100; [2014] 2 P & CR 8 at paragraph 30.

> *buildings erected on the site and, similarly, any new fixtures that may be installed on the site."*

194. Rimer LJ went onto to recognise in that case that the critical question was whether the clause in issue was *"in fact to be interpreted as intending to refer to the new building and fixtures"*, which was a question of construction.[278]

195. The principle is therefore that a covenant to repair premises will apply to any subsequent alteration or addition unless that outcome is excluded by the language used.[279] *Hyman v Rose*[280] is an example of where the language of the lease departed from this general rule, where the removal of a wall and iron railings was found not to be a breach of the obligation to repair and maintain the demised premises, as the wall and railings had not been shown to be present at the date of the demise and the covenant did not apply to them.[281]

<u>Interpretation of alteration covenants</u>

196. The approach taken by the courts to the interpretation of leases has been set out in chapter 1. Those principles are applicable to the interpretation of alteration covenants. When interpreting an alterations clause, as with any other clause, the task of the court is to identify the intention of the parties by reference to what a reasonable person, having all the background knowledge which would have been available to the parties, would have understood them to be using the language in the clause to mean, having regard to:

---

[278] As above, the court in *Never-Stop Railway (Wembley) Ltd v British Empire Exhibition (1924) Inc* [1926] Ch 877 likewise recognised that the principle was subject to any agreement to the contrary.

[279] See further *Field v Curnick* [1926] 2 KB 374 at 378-379.

[280] [1912] AC 623.

[281] See 632.

a) The natural and ordinary meaning of the clause;

b) Any other relevant provisions of the contract;

c) The overall purpose of the clause and the contract;

d) The facts and circumstances known or assumed by the parties at the time that the document was executed;

e) Commercial common sense.

Structural vs non-structural alterations

197. Alteration clauses are frequently drafted so as to draw a distinction between structural and non-structural alterations. In any given case, what is meant by 'structural' must be assessed by reading the lease as a whole. Each case will turn on the drafting of the particular lease and there is not a definition of 'structural' which applies for all purposes[282].

198. Subject to that caveat, case law suggests that permanent alterations or additions to the fabric of the building (whether or not load bearing) are likely to be structural alterations. For example:

a) In *Pearlman v Keepers and Governors of Harrow School*[283], finding the installation of central heating to be a *"structural alteration, extension or addition"* under the Housing Act 1974, the Court of Appeal observed that 'structural', in that context, meant *"something which involves the fabric of the house as opposed to the provision merely of a piece of equipment"*, it

[282] A point emphasised by the court in *Riva Properties Limited v Staghold (Birmingham) Limited* [2004] EWHC 3376 (Ch) at paragraphs 20-22.

[283] [1979] QB 56 (CA).

mattering not *"whether the fabric in question is load-bearing"*[284].

b) In *Irvine v Moran*[285] (1992) 24 HLR 1, considering what amounts to the structure of a dwelling house for the purposes of s32 of the Housing Act 1961, which imposed a duty on lessors to keep the structure in repair, the judge concluded that:

"...the structure of the dwellinghouse consists of those elements of the overall dwellinghouse which give it its essential appearance, stability and shape. The expression does not extend to the many and various ways in which the dwellinghouse will be fitted out, equipped, decorated and generally made to be habitable. I am not persuaded...that one should limit the expression "the structure of the dwellinghouse" to those aspects of the dwellinghouse which are load bearing... but what I do feel is, as regards the words "structure of the dwellinghouse", that in order to be part of the structure of the dwellinghouse a particular element must be a material or significant element in the overall construction."[286]

c) In *Riva Properties Limited v Staghold (Birmingham) Limited*[287], the court cited approvingly commentary that the structure of a modern office building will normally include:

   i. The steel frame and roof;

[284] At 72G (per Geoffrey Lane LJ). See, to like effect, 67C (Lord Denning MR) and 79B (Eveleigh LJ): *"In my opinion structural means appertaining to the fabric of a building so as to be a part of the complex whole"*

[285] (1992) 24 HLR 1.

[286] At 5.

[287] [2004] EWHC 3376 (Ch).

ii. The concrete infills in the walls and the prefabricated cladding which keep out the elements, despite being non-load bearing;

iii. The concrete floors.

199. Raised floors, built on top of the concrete base, are perhaps less likely to be structural – it will depend upon the circumstances and the drafting of the particular lease. In *Bent v High Cliff Developments Limited*[288] the court, after considering the *Pearlman* and *Irvine* cases, concluded on the drafting of the particular lease that the replacement of steel windows with aluminium windows did not amount to a structural alteration[289].

Landlord and tenant fixtures, chattels, fittings

200. An issue which sometimes arises is whether a particular item is (1) an integral part of the demised building/land; (2) a fixture (of either the landlord or the tenant) or (3) a chattel[290]. The answer may determine whether a tenant:

a) May alter the item during the term;

b) May remove the item at the end of the term;

c) Must yield the item up in a condition compliant with a tenant repairing covenant.

---

[288] (1999) 96(34) LSG 35.

[289] See paragraphs 27-34.

[290] As to this threefold classification, see *Marlborough Knightsbridge Management Ltd v Fivaz* [2021] EWCA Civ 989; [2021] 1 WLR 4345 at paragraph 15.

When is an item a fixture?

201. Any item is which is a fundamental/integral part of the thing demised is not a fixture. In *Boswell v Crucible Steel Company*[291], the Court of Appeal considered whether large plate glass windows were landlord fixtures for the purpose of a tenant repairing covenant. Finding that they a fundamental part of the thing demised and not landlord fixtures, Scrutton LJ said that the expression 'landlord fixtures':

> *"...cannot include a thing which forms part of the original structure of the building. It must be regarded as confined to things which have been brought into the house and affixed to the freehold after the structure is completed. If these windows could be treated as landlord's fixtures, the whole house would be a landlord's fixture."*[292]

202. Atkins LJ was of the same view, holding that the windows:

> *"...are not fixtures at all in the sense in which that term is generally understood. A fixture, as that term is used in connection with a house, means something which has been affixed to the freehold as accessory to the house. It does not include things which were made part of the house itself in the course of its construction. And the expression "landlord's fixtures," as I understand it, covers all those chattels which have been so affixed by way of addition to the original structure, and were so affixed either by the landlord, or, if by the tenant, under circumstances in which they were not removable by him. As these windows were part of the original structure, representing the walls of the house, so that without them there would be nothing that could be described as a warehouse at all, they cannot come under the head of landlord's fixtures. If they could, every brick used in the building would be a landlord's fixture."*[293]

---

291 [1925] 1 KB 119.

292 At 122.

293 At 123.

203. *Boswell v Crucible Steel Company* was recently applied by the Court of Appeal in *Marlborough Knightsbridge Management Ltd v Fivaz*[294]. In that case, the tenant owned two flats within a block, with each lease containing a tenant covenant not to *"remove any of the landlords fixtures"* without consent. The tenant replaced the entrance doors to the flats without seeking consent and the issue for the court was whether that breached the covenant. The Court of Appeal upheld the judgment of the Upper Tribunal that there had been no breach as the entrance doors were not landlord fixtures. Giving the judgment of the court, Arnold LJ cited the above comments of Scrutton LJ and Atkins LJ in *Boswell* and found the case to be indistinguishable to the facts before the court, continuing that:

> *"…The entrance doors in the present case were part of the original structure of the flats. Moreover, they were an essential part of the structure, since they afforded privacy and security to the tenant(s). It is no doubt true that the doors were affixed to the walls (via door frames) by hinges after the walls were built, but that is immaterial. No one would say that the construction of a flat was complete if the entrance door had not yet been hung."*

204. On this approach, a fixture is something which has been affixed to the demised land or building in such a way that it can no longer be considered a chattel, but has not become an integral part of the building.

Landlord fixtures

205. Because of the way the common law has evolved, 'landlord fixtures' are a difficult concept. Originally, at common law, everything other than chattels that was affixed to leasehold property became part of it. The consequence was that such items became the property of the landlord, even if affixed by and previously the property of the tenant, and could not be removed by the tenant at the end of the

[294] [2021] EWCA Civ 989; [2021] 1 WLR 4345.

term[295]. The injustice of that rule led to the eventual recognition of tenant fixtures, being those fixtures which, absent some provision to the contrary in the lease, could be removed by the tenant at the end of the term. The distinction was thus between (1) items which formed part of the property itself, whether as originally demised or by annexation; (2) tenant fixtures which could be removed and (3) chattels which never became part of the property at all. The distinction was recognised by the Court of Exchequer Chamber in *Climie v Wood*[296], where Willes J explained:

"There is no doubt that sometimes things annexed to land remain chattels as much after they have been annexed as they were before. The case of pictures hung on a wall for the purpose of being more conveniently seen may be mentioned by way of illustration. On the other hand, things may be made so completely a part of the land, as being essential to its convenient use, that even a tenant could not remove them. An example of this class of chattel may be found in doors or windows. Lastly, things may be annexed to land, for the purposes of trade or of domestic convenience or ornament, in so permanent a manner as really to form a part of the land; and yet the tenant who has erected them is entitled to remove them during his term, or, it may be, within a reasonable time after its expiration."[297]

206. Viewed in that way, conceptually there does not appear to be much room for a fourth category of 'landlord fixtures' and the term has attracted judicial criticism.[298] This was noted by the Court of

[295] See *Marlborough Knightsbridge Management Ltd v Fivaz* [2021] EWCA Civ 989; [2021] 1 WLR 4345 at paragraph 13.

[296] (1869) LR 4 Exch 328.

[297] At 329-330. This passage was cited by the Court of Appeal in *Marlborough Knightsbridge Management Ltd v Fivaz* [2021] EWCA Civ 989; [2021] 1 WLR 4345 at paragraph 17.

[298] In *Elliott v Bishop* (1854) 10 Ex 496 at 508 Martin B described the expression as *"a most inaccurate one"*. In *Lambourn v McLellan* [1903] 2 Ch 268 at 274 Vaughan Williams LJ said that it was *"not a happy expression"*. In *Boswell v Crucible Steel Co* [1925] 1 KB 119 at 122 Scrutton LJ said that

Appeal in *Marlborough Knightsbridge Management Ltd v Fivaz* which proceeded on the *"generally accepted"* basis that landlord fixtures are simply those fixtures which are not tenant fixtures[299].

Tenant fixtures

207. As explained above, where a tenant pays for and/or installs an item which becomes a fundamental part of the building, it will not be a fixture at all (tenant or landlord). For example, in *South Essex Partnership University NHS Foundation Trust v Laindon Holdings Ltd*[300], the Court of Appeal held that the installation of lifts, although paid for by the tenant, on any view became *"become part of the fabric of the Building, rather than a fixture"*[301].

208. Subject to that caveat, tenant fixtures are those fixtures which, subject to the terms of the lease, are removeable by the tenant. To be a tenant fixture:

a) The fixture must have been annexed by or on behalf of the tenant, not the landlord; and

b) Be one of the three recognised categories of tenant fixtures. These are (i) trade fixtures; (ii) ornamental and domestic fixtures and (iii) agricultural fixtures.

209. Trade fixtures are those items which have been attached by the tenant in order to enable them to carry on their trade or business at the premises. The policy behind allowing trade fixtures to be

---

he had *"always had a difficulty in understanding what is meant by 'landlord's fixtures'."*

[299] [2021] EWCA Civ 989; [2021] 1 WLR 4345 at paragraph 12.

[300] [2016] EWCA Civ 377; [2016] L & TR 30.

[301] Paragraph 10.

removed is that, in the absence of such a rule, the law would disincentivise tenants from laying out money to improve land.[302]

210. Further, to be a tenant fixture the item must:

a) Be possible to remove without causing substantial damage to the land[303]. This is a question of fact and degree;

b) Once removed, retain is essential character and utility[304]. This is unlikely to be the case unless, following removal, the item is capable of being set up and used elsewhere.

211. It should also be kept in mind that:

a) Fixtures which are installed by the tenant to replace fixtures belonging to the landlord do not become tenant fixtures and are not removeable[305];

b) The tenant's right to remove tenant fixtures may be restricted or varied by the terms of the lease;

c) The tenant may remove its fixtures during its tenancy. Where a tenancy ends by effluxion of time and the tenant vacates without removing its fixtures, the right to do so is lost[306];

d) As fixtures become part of the demised premises, unless the lease requires the tenant to remove its fixtures at the end of

---

302 As was recognised by the court in *Penton v Robart* (1801) 2 East 88 at 90.

303 *Spyer v Phillipson* [1931] 2 Ch. 183 at 209-210.

304 *Webb v Frank Bevis Ltd* [1940] 1 All ER 247.

305 See *Sunderland v Newton* (1830) 3 Simons 450.

306 *Lyde v Russell* (1830) 1 B. & Ad. 394, where it was explained (at 396) that *"the property in fixtures, which would be in the tenant if he removed them during the term, vests in the landlord on the determination of the term."*

term, the tenant may but is not required to do so[307]. This is in contrast to the position for chattels, which do not become part of the property and must be removed as part of the tenant's obligation to yield up the premises with vacant possession;

e) The tenant must make good any damage caused as a result of the removal of the tenant fixtures.

Chattels

212. Anything which is neither an integral part of the demised property nor a fixture is a chattel. Unlike fixtures, chattels do not become part of the property. A common example is furniture. Affixation to the property is a weighty factor, but is not conclusive, as to whether an items has lost its chattel nature. For example, cinema seats have been held to chattels despite a degree of affixation.[308]

213. The tenant may remove its chattels at any time and must have removed them by the end of the term in order to yield up the premises with vacant possession.

Fittings

214. While many commercial leases refer to 'fittings', normally in combination with 'fixtures', it is not a legal term of art[309] and its meaning will depend upon the drafting of the particular lease.

[307] *See Never-Stop Railway (Wembley) Ltd v British Empire Exhibition (1924) Inc* [1926] Ch 877 at 885; *Legal & General Assurance Society Ltd v Expeditors International (UK) Ltd* [2007] 1 P & CR 5 at paragraph 32] (on appeal: [2007] EWCA Civ 7; [2007] 2 P & CR 10).

[308] *Lyon v London & Midland Bank* [1903] 2 KB 135.

[309] A point made by Newey J in *Earl of Cardigan v Moore* [2012] EWHC 1024 (Ch) at paragraph 37.

Depending on the drafting, it may be a term for fixtures, fixtures and chattels or just chattels.

Alterations: terms implied at common law

Implied restrictions on undertaking alterations

215. The approach taken by the courts to the implication of terms has been set out in chapter 2. As discussed above in the context of waste, there is a line of authority supporting the implication of an obligation on the tenant to use the premises in a 'tenant like manner', arising from the nature of the landlord/tenant relationship[310]. The content of the duty has been set out above.

216. Although the case law on the obligation to use the premises in a tenant like manner pre-dates the case law on the modern approach to the implication of terms, it is considered that it likely continues to be applicable. As an implied term, the obligation will yield to any inconsistent provision made by the lease.

217. Beyond that obligation, it is considered unlikely that further restrictions upon tenant alterations will meet the tests of necessity or obviousness which apply to implied terms. Where the law already imposes obligations not to commit voluntary waste, and where there is the implied obligation of tenant like user, it will be difficult to argue that without further restrictions on alterations a lease would lack commercial coherence, or that any particular form of additional restriction is so obvious that it goes without saying.

Alterations: terms implied by statute - section 19(2) of the Landlord and Tenant Act 1927

218. Section 19(2) of the Landlord and Tenant Act 1927 provides that:

[310] See for example *Marsden v Edward Heyes Ltd* [1927] 2 KB 1; *Warren v Keen* [1954] 1 QB 15.

> *"In all leases whether made before or after the commencement of this Act containing a covenant condition or agreement against the making of improvements without a licence or consent, such covenant condition or agreement shall be deemed, notwithstanding any express provision to the contrary, to be subject to a proviso that such licence or consent is not to be unreasonably withheld; but this proviso does not preclude the right to require as a condition of such licence or consent the payment of a reasonable sum in respect of any damage to or diminution in the value of the premises or any neighbouring premises belonging to the landlord, and of any legal or other expenses properly incurred in connection with such licence or consent nor, in the case of an improvement which does not add to the letting value of the holding, does it preclude the right to require as a condition of such licence or consent, where such a requirement would be reasonable, an undertaking on the part of the tenant to reinstate the premises in the condition in which they were before the improvement was executed."*

219. It should be noted that:

a) The application of s19(2) is limited to covenants against the making of improvements, it does not apply to every restriction on alterations;

b) Section 19(2) only applies to covenants against making alterations without licence or consent, it does not apply to absolute covenants against improvements[311];

c) Where s19(2) applies, the parties cannot contract out of the obligation as it applies "*notwithstanding any express provision to the contrary*".

---

[311] In *F. W. Woolworth and Company Ltd v Lambert* [1937] Ch 37, the argument was advanced that s19(1) applied to absolute covenants. The Court of Appeal rejected that argument on the basis that such a construction *"would be to disregard the words of the section altogether—namely, the words 'without licence or consent.'"* It is considered that the same applies to s19(2).

220. The effect of s19(2), for those covenants to which is applies, is to upgrade partially qualified covenants into fully qualified covenants.

What is an improvement for the purposes of section 19(2)?

221. It was held by the majority of the Court of Appeal in *F. W. Woolworth and Company, Limited v Lambert*[312] that:

a) Whether an alteration is an improvement is judged from the point of view of the tenant[313];

b) An alteration will be an improvement if it increases the benefit which the tenant obtains in its use of the premises.[314] This could include alterations to enable the premises to be used with adjoining premises also in the tenant's control.[315]

Burden of proof under s19(2)

222. The burden of showing that consent has been unreasonably withheld under s19(2) is upon the tenant[316]. There is no equivalent of s1(6) of the Landlord and Tenant Act 1988 reversing the burden of proof.

---

312 [1937] Ch 37, Lord Wright MR and Romer LJ in the majority, with Greene LJ dissenting.

313 Pg49 per Lord Wright MR. See too pg55-56, per Romer LJ.

314 Pgs49-50 per Lord Wright MR. At pg56, per Romer LJ put the question as whether the alterations *"render the tenants' occupation of the demised premises more convenient and comfortable to them?"*

315 Pgs49-50 per Lord Wright MR.

316 See *F. W. Woolworth and Company, Limited v Lambert* [1937] Ch 37 at 42 (Lord Wright MR); 55 (Romer LJ) and 61 (Greene LJ).

Implied limits on a landlord's discretion under a partially qualified covenant against alterations

223. It is considered unlikely that the tests of business efficacy or obviousness will be often met in order to upgrade (by the implication of words) an absolute covenant against alterations into a qualified covenant.

224. Where the covenant against alterations is partially qualified, for improvements the covenant will be upgraded into a fully qualified covenant by s19(2) of the Landlord and Tenant Act 1927.

225. The limits imposed upon a landlord's discretion under a partially qualified covenant are discussed in chapter 6.

Fully qualified covenants: the reasonableness test

226. The approach of the courts when assessing whether a landlord has reasonably withheld consent to alterations and/or improvements are discussed in detail in chapter 6. The relevant principles were helpful summarised by the Court of Appeal in *Iqbal v Thakrar*[317].

Consequences of the landlord failing to act reasonably in withholding consent

227. Where a tenant considers that their landlord has unreasonably refused consent to proposed improvements under a fully qualified covenant, the tenant may seek a declaration from the court that consent has been unreasonably withheld[318].

228. Where a tenant considers that their landlord has unreasonably refused consent to proposed alterations or improvements under a fully qualified covenant, provided the tenant is right, and provided that the alterations do not breach the lease in some way, the tenant

---

317 [2004] EWCA Civ 592; [2004] 3 EGLR 21 at paragraph 26.

318 The County Court has jurisdiction to hear such a claim: s53(1)(b) of the Landlord and Tenant Act 1954.

may proceed to make the alterations without consent and to do so will not breach the covenant.[319]

229. Both of these possibilities, and the underlying case law, are discussed in detail in chapter 8. Seeking a declaration from the court, prior to altering the demised premises, is ordinarily the safer if slower option.

Tenant obligations at the end of the term: reinstating the premises

230. Commercial leases usually make express provision for the reinstatement of the premises at the end of the term. That obligation will sometimes include the removal of tenant alterations.

231. The required condition of the property at the end of the term will also be governed by the tenant repairing covenants and, potentially, by the obligation in the tort of waste to make good any damage caused by the removal of tenant fixtures.

Express obligations to reinstate

232. Tenant covenants to reinstate the premises can be:

a) Absolute, requiring reinstatement without any requirement for prior notice from the landlord; or

b) More commonly, dependent on prior notice from the landlord that reinstatement is required. Where reinstatement is conditional upon prior notice, in the absence of a valid notice served in the accordance with the requirements of the lease, no liability to reinstate arises.

233. For covenants to reinstate which are dependent upon notice, two issues can arise: (1) what form any notice to reinstate must take and (2) how much notice must be given.

---

[319] See *F. W. Woolworth and Company Limited v Lambert* [1937] Ch 37 at 53.

What form must notice take?

234. This will turn upon the interpretation of the document imposing the obligation. Oral notice is, in principle, acceptable[320] but it will often be precluded by the drafting, in particular the terms governing the service of notices.

235. Unless the lease provides otherwise, no particular form of notice to reinstate is required, all that is needed is that a reasonable tenant would understand that the landlord is requiring reinstatement. There are cases in which a schedule of dilapidations has been held to be sufficient notice to reinstate, even where the schedule did not explicitly refer to the licence for alterations.[321] Relying on the schedule of dilapidations can, however, be high risk. The schedule may not be sufficiently clear that reinstatement is being required and may be served at a time when the right to require reinstatement has already passed. A separate notice requiring restatement will usually be advisable.

236. Dependent on the drafting of the lease/licence for alterations, a notice will not be invalided by the fact that certain aspects of the reinstatement works fall to be agreed with the landlord or their representatives[322] after the notice has been given.[323]

---

[320] For an example of where oral notice was sufficient, see *L Batley Pet Products Ltd v North Lanarkshire Council* [2014] UKSC 27; [2014] 3 All ER 64 paragraphs 16, 19-20 and 23-25.

[321] See for example *Westminster City Council v HSBC Bank Plc* [2003] 1 EGLR 62 paragraphs 48-50.

[322] Likely the landlord's surveyor.

[323] See, for example, *Fairgate International Ltd v Citibank International Plc* (2006) 1 P & CR 2 at paragraph 26 where the Court of Appeal rejected an argument that such a notice was void for uncertainty.

How much notice is required?

237. The lease or licence for alterations may specify an end date by which notice to reinstate must have been given. In such a case, a court is likely to interpret time as being of the essence.

238. Where the lease/licence is silent on the time by which notice to reinstate must have been given, it is anticipated that the correct interpretation will usually be that any notice must, as a minimum, be given before the determination of the lease. Any other interpretation would allow the obligation to arise after the tenant has already been required to yield up possession in accordance with the covenants, and where the tenant is no longer in a position to be able to perform the obligation.

239. A further issue is whether *sufficient* notice to reinstate must be given. For example, if the tenant is given notice to reinstate the day before the term expires, is that valid notice?

240. It is thought that the answer will depend upon the drafting of the particular agreement – there are broadly three possibilities[324]:

a) That, for the notice to be valid, the tenant must be given sufficient notice that a reasonable tenant could undertake the necessary works within the remaining lease term;

b) That notice may be given at any time prior to the determination of the lease but that the tenant is entitled following the notice to remain in occupation for a reasonable period to complete the works, even if that period postdates the expiry of the term;

c) That notice may be given at any time prior to the determination of the term, whether or not that allows the

---

[324] For a detailed discussion of each possibility and the case law see Dilapidations: The Modern Law and Practice (7th. Ed) (Dowding K.C., Reynolds K.C., Oakes) at 16-06 to 16-07.

tenant sufficient time to compete the works before the term expires. If it does not, the tenant will be in breach of the obligation to reinstate.

241. The third possibility has the advantage that, unlike the first and second possibilities, it does not require the implication of further terms. However, it is thought that a court will be reluctant to adopt this interpretation, as it allows a consciousness tenant to be placed in breach of its obligations through no fault of its own. Further, if the tenant pre-emptively removed the alterations, that itself would (absent notice to reinstate) likely be a breach of covenant - as explained above the alterations will have become part of the demised premises and so become subject to the covenants against alterations and to yield up the premises at the end of the term.

242. As for the first and second possibilities, such case law as there is supports the second possibility ordinarily being the correct one: i.e. that following the notice to reinstate the tenant may remain in occupation for a reasonable period to complete the works, even if that period postdates the expiry of the term. In *Matthey v Curling*[325], Lord Atkinson observed that:

"...in the case of an ordinary covenant to reinstate, a covenantor shall in the absence of words expressly or impliedly fixing a time for the performance of his covenant, have what is a reasonable time under all the circumstances of the case for its performance, whether, in the case of a leasehold, that time extends beyond the term or the contrary."[326]

---

[325] [1922] 2 AC 180.

[326] At 240. These comments were later cited by the High Court in *Baroque Investments v Heis* [2012] EWHC 2886 (Ch); (2013) 1 P & CR 11, where the tenant had covenanted 'before the end of the lease' to reinstate the premises. The court accepted the submission that, absent the words 'before the end of the lease', the tenant *"would have a reasonable time after its termination to carry out the reinstatement works"* – see paragraphs 7-8.

243. It is an area of uncertainty, where this occurs, on what basis and subject to what terms the tenant remains in occupation and in particular whether any rent is payable.

Limits on a landlord's ability to require reinstatement

244. The covenant to reinstate may impose express limits upon the landlord's ability to require reinstatement, for example that it may only be required where reasonable.

245. Where there are no express limitations, as is explained in chapter 6, there is a line of case law that where a contract bestows upon one of the parties a contractual discretion which affects the rights of both parties, that discretion is subject to an implied limitation that it must be exercised rationally, in good faith and consistent with its contractual purpose.[327] It is certainly arguable that the ability to require reinstatement is such a discretion and so is subject to those implied limitations.

Covenants requiring reinstatement unless the landlord requires otherwise

246. Where a covenant provides for reinstatement unless the landlord requires otherwise, towards the end of the term the tenant is faced with the difficult choice whether to (1) begin reinstating but with the risk that the landlord subsequently gives notice reinstatement is not required or (2) delay reinstating which risks there being insufficient time to comply with the obligation to reinstate in the event no notice is given. One possible option for a tenant in this situation is to ask the landlord to confirm whether reinstatement is required and, if so, to what extent, as well as to give the landlord notice that it intends to commence reinstating the premises.

---

[327] See *Braganza v BP Shopping Ltd* [2015] UKSC 17; [2015] 1 WLR 1661 at paragraph 30; *Waaler v Hounslow London Borough Council* [2017] EWCA Civ 45; [2017] 1 WLR 2817 at paragraph 20.

247. If a tenant reinstates in accordance with the covenant, a landlord which knew of the reinstatement works and did not object, and then afterwards gave notice that the premises was not to be reinstated, would likely face arguments from the tenant that:

a) Reinstatement works prior to notice being given cannot be retrospectively made a breach of covenant by later notice; and/or

b) There is an implied term that notice reinstatement is not required should be given within a reasonable time before the end of the term. What is a reasonable time will include the landlord's knowledge that the tenant is about the commence reinstatement works; and/or

c) Potentially, that the landlord is now estopped from serving notice that the premises should not be reinstated.

What amounts to reinstatement

248. What amounts to reinstatement will depend upon the drafting of the covenant in question. Generally, it will involve:

a) Removing the alterations;

b) Making good any damage caused by the removal;

c) Reinstating what was there previously.

Alterations made under previous leases

249. Where a tenant occupies under two successive leases and alterations were made during the term of the first lease and were not reinstated prior to the commencement of the second lease, then the default position is that the alterations became part of the thing originally demised by the second lease, to be yielded up at the end of the term

(rather than reinstated)[328]. However, this will yield to any clause to the contrary, either expressly or by implication.

Obligation of successors in title to reinstate

250. As is discussed in chapter 3, for 'new tenancies', the provisions of the Landlord and Tenant (Covenants) Act 1995 ("LTCA 1995") apply to the tenant covenants in both the tenancy itself and any collateral agreements[329]. A 'tenant covenant' is a *"a covenant falling to be complied with by the tenant of premises demised by the tenancy"*. Covenants to reinstate contained within a licence to assign are, therefore, caught by the LTCA 1995. The consequence is that both the benefit and the burden of the covenant to reinstate passes upon an assignment of the tenancy, and upon a landlord assignment of the reversion[330].

251. An exception will be where the covenant is, in whatever terms, *"expressed to be personal to any person"*[331].

Where the lease is silent on reinstatement

Lawful alterations

252. Where a lease is silent on alterations, as discussed above, the tenant is free to alter the premises as it sees fit, subject to limitations imposed:

---

[328] Ordinarily, and subject to any drafting to the contrary, a covenant in the second lease against making alterations would be judged against the condition of the premises as it stood at the date of the second lease, not at some earlier time.

[329] Section 28(1) defines 'covenant' as including any *"term, condition and obligation"* and states that references to a covenant of a tenancy *"include a covenant…contained in a collateral agreement"*;

[330] See s3(1)(b) of the LTCA 1995.

[331] Section 3(6)(a) of the LTCA 1995.

a) By the tort of voluntary waste;

b) By the implied obligation to use the premises in a tenant like manner;

c) By the other covenants in the lease, in particular the covenants of repair.

253. If the alterations do not breach any of those restrictions, the alterations are not a breach of the lease and the landlord will have no remedy in respect of them.

254. Nor will the landlord have the right to require their reinstatement: they become part of the demised premises and the tenant may yield them up, they are not required to remove them.[332]

Unlawful alterations

255. Where a tenant undertakes alterations in breach of covenant the landlord may bring a claim against the tenant for that breach.

256. Whether a covenant to reinstate alterations extends to unauthorised alterations will turn upon the drafting of the particular covenant. If it does not, as with lawful alterations, the rule is that the alterations become part of the property and the tenant will not liable to remove them at the expiry of the lease. The landlord will, however, have a claim against the tenant for the undertaking the alterations in breach of covenant in the first place.[333]

Remedies for failure to reinstate

257. The question of what remedies are available to a landlord against a tenant's breach of covenant are discussed in chapter 8. Where there has been a failure to reinstate, a landlord's primary remedy will be

---

[332] See, for example, *Never-Stop Railway (Wembley) Ltd v British Empire Exhibition (1924) Inc* [1926] Ch 877 at 885.

[333] Subject to limitation issues and being able to prove loss.

a claim in damages for the breach of covenant. Although the court has jurisdiction to grant a mandatory injunction requiring the tenant to undertake the works, it is considered unlikely that this remedy would be granted where the landlord can be adequately compensated in damages.

Summary

258. The relevant principles can be summarised as follows:

a) At common law, a tenant has the right to alter the demised premises as an incident of their rights of ownership. That right is, however, subject to the tenant covenants in the lease and the obligation in tort not to commit voluntary waste;

b) Most commercial leases make detailed provision for the condition of the premises and tortious claims for voluntary waste are rare;

c) It is a general rule of the common law that anything which is attached to land becomes part of it. In the leasehold context, things attached to the demised premises (i.e. alterations, additions) become part of them and references in a lease to the 'demised premises' will ordinarily be taken to include them. If so, the tenant repairing covenants will apply to any alterations / additions made, unless that outcome is excluded by the language used;

d) Alteration clauses are frequently drafted so as to draw a distinction between structural and non-structural alterations. In any given case, what is meant by 'structural' must be assessed by reading the lease as a whole – there is no single definition of 'structural' which applies for all purposes. Subject to that caveat, case law suggests that permanent alterations or additions to the fabric of the building (whether or not load bearing) are likely to be structural alterations;

e) For improvements, s19(2) of the Landlord and Tenant Act 1927 upgrades partially qualified covenants into fully qualified covenants. The section applies "*notwithstanding any express provision to the contrary*";

f) The burden of showing that consent has been unreasonably withheld under s19(2) is upon the tenant;

g) Where a lease makes the reinstatement of alterations dependent on prior notice from the landlord, in the absence of a valid notice served in the accordance with the requirements of the lease, no tenant liability to reinstate arises.

CHAPTER FIVE

RULES GOVERNING USER COVENANTS

259. The uses to which demises premises may be put, or may not be put, is a central concern of both landlords and tenants and is almost invariably expressly provided for in commercial leases.

Restrictions on user imposed by planning law

260. External to the terms of the lease, the uses to which premises may be put are also government by planning law[334]. The modern planning framework is primarily statute based, the main sources being the Town and Country Planning Act 1990, together with the Town and Country Planning (Use Classes) Order 1987 and:

a) For England, the Town and Country Planning (General Permitted Development) (England) Order 2015;

b) For Wales, the Town and Country Planning (General Permitted Development) Order 1995.

261. Planning controls operate independently of the controls on user imposed by leases. So, it is no defence to a breach of planning control that the use is permitted under a tenant's lease, nor is it any defence to an action for breach of a user covenant that the tenant obtained planning permission for the use in question.

[334] For the workings of the planning system, reference should be made to specialist works.

Landlord obligations relevant to the user of the premises

Fitness of the demised premises for particular uses

262. In general, the common law will not imply a term into a lease that the demised premises are fit for any particular use or can be lawfully put to any particular use. The general principle is 'caveat lessee': the tenant takes the premises as they find them.

263. There are exceptions to this principle, including where a property is let furnished and where a landlord retains property which is essential to access the demised premises[335]. Statute has also intervened concerning the condition of residential property.

No warranty demised premises fit for any particular use

264. In *Hart v Windsor*[336], Parke B held that *"There is no contract, still less a condition, implied by law on the demise of real property only, that it is fit for the purpose for which it is let. The principles of the common law do not warrant such a position."*[337]

265. These comments were subsequently cited by Scrutton LJ in *Bottomley v Bannister*[338], who held that it was:

> *"...well established English law that, in the absence of express contract, a landlord of an unfurnished house is not liable to his tenant, or a vendor of real estate to his purchaser, for defects in the house or land*

[335] See *Liverpool CC v Irwin* [1977] AC 239.

[336] (1843) 12 M & W 68.

[337] At 87.

[338] [1932] 1 KB 458.

rendering it dangerous or unfit for occupation, even if he has constructed the defects himself or is aware of their existence."[339]

266. Scrutton LJ then:

a) Referred to *Sutton v Temple*[340] (1843) 12 M. & W. 52 where the same conclusion was reached for a lease of grazing land;

b) Observed that whether the law should be otherwise was a matter for Parliament.[341]

No warranty demised premises may be lawfully put to a particular use

267. In *Edler* v *Auerbach*[342], Devlin J referred back to the comments of Parke B in *Hart v Windsor* and found them to be *"equally applicable where premises are, so to speak, legally unfit"*. For Devlin J:

"It is the business of the tenant, if he does not protect himself by an express warranty, to satisfy himself that the premises are fit for the purpose for which he wants to use them, whether that fitness depends upon the state of their structure, the state of the law, or any other relevant circumstances."[343]

268. The court returned to this issue in *Hills v Harris*[344], where a sub-lease required the tenant not to carry on any noisy trade or business other than that of a confectionery and tobacco retailer. The head lease limited the premises to use for boot and shoe making. The sub-tenant used the premises for the sale of tobacco and the head

---

339 468. Statute has since intervened in the context of residential property. For dangerous defects, the provisions of the Defective Premises Act 1972 might also be engaged.

340 (1843) 12 M & W 52.

341 469.

342 [1950] 1 K.B. 359.

343 374.

344 [1965] 2 Q.B. 601.

landlord intervened to prohibit its sale from the shop. The sub-tenant claimed damages from their landlord for breach of an implied warranty that the premises could be used for the sale of tobacco. The Court of Appeal rejected there being any such warranty, with Diplock LJ approving Devlin J's summary of the law in *Edler* v *Auerbach* set out above[345] . It did not matter whether or not the lease was entered into in the contemplation of both parties that the property would be used for the sale of tobacco.

269. Russell LJ added that to find that the circumstances amounted to an express warranty would *"fly in the face of the principle exemplified in Edler v Auerbach"*. A warranty did not arise out of *"the mere fact that both sides appeared to assume that a particular use would be made of the premises."*[346]

270. The principle was upheld again in *Molton Builders Ltd v Westminster LBC*[347]. There, the Crown Estate Commissions let a suit of rooms with a covenant restricting the user to *"private dwelling houses, first class clubs or residential or professional chambers or offices only"*. The premises was used as private residences until part was sublet and, without planning permission, used as offices. The Crown Estate Commissioners gave their consent to the service of an enforcement notice by the local planning authority. The sub-tenant sought a declaration that the giving of consent to the service of the enforcement notice amounted to a derogation from grant.

271. The claim failed. Denning M.R.:

a) Held that the principle of non-derogation from grant is a *"general principle of law that, if one man agrees to confer a particular benefit on another, he must not do anything which substantially deprives the other of the enjoyment of that benefit:*

---

[345] 615.

[346] 617.

[347] (1975) 30 P & CR 183.

because that would be to take away with one hand what is given with the other"[348];

b) It is, properly understood, not an implied term of the contract but a *"principle evolved by the law itself"*[349] and an *"independent rule of law"*[350];

c) However, it did not benefit the sub-tenant in that case because:

"When a man sells or lets land for a particular purpose, it is always subject to the proviso that it is lawful to carry on that purpose. Neither the buyer nor the tenant can pray in aid the doctrine of derogation from grant so as to enable him to do something which is unlawful."[351]

Interpretation of express user covenants

272. The principles governing the interpretation of leases have been set out in chapter 1. Those principles apply to the interpretation of user covenants.

273. It is common for user covenants in leases to restrict the use of premises to one or more of the use classes specified in the Town and Country Planning (Use Classes) Order 1987. Whether such a reference is to the Use Classes Order as in force at the date of the lease, of as amended from time to time, is a question of interpretation. Where one of the objectives of a user covenant is to ensure the premises is used in a way which does not breach planning control, the latter interpretation is perhaps the more likely.

---

[348] 186.

[349] 186.

[350] 187.

[351] 187.

274. Where there is no user covenant, using the premises in a way which is a breach of planning control may in any event breach a covenant to comply with the requirements of statute.

Terms relevant to user implied at common law

275. As discussed in chapter 4, there are cases in which the court has held tenants to be under an implied duty to act in a tenant like manner. As discussed there, the content and scope of this duty are uncertain, but such case law as there is has tied the duty to not making structural alterations which substantially change the character of the premises and generally taking care of premises rather than governing the actual uses made of premises by tenants.

Terms implied by statute

276. Section 19(3) of the Landlord and Tenant Act 1927 provides that:

In all leases whether made before or after the commencement of this Act containing a covenant condition or agreement against the alteration of the user of the demised premises, without licence or consent, such covenant condition or agreement shall, if the alteration does not involve any structural alteration of the premises, be deemed, notwithstanding any express provision to the contrary, to be subject to a proviso that no fine or sum of money in the nature of a fine, whether by way of increase of rent or otherwise, shall be payable for or in respect of such licence or consent; but this proviso does not preclude the right of the landlord to require payment of a reasonable sum in respect of any damage to or diminution in the value of the premises or any neighbouring premises belonging to him and of any legal or other expenses incurred in connection with such licence or consent.

Where a dispute as to the reasonableness of any such sum has been determined by a court of competent jurisdiction, the landlord shall be bound to grant the licence or consent on payment of the sum so determined to be reasonable.

277. It should be noted that s19(3):

a) Only applies to qualified covenants, not to absolute covenants as absolute covenants do not restrict alterations of user *"without licence or consent"*[352];

b) Does not apply if the alteration of user involves any structural alteration to the premises;

c) Does not upgrade a partially qualified covenant into a fully qualified covenant, it merely prohibits the taking of a fine as a condition of consent;

d) The landlord may, however, require payment of a reasonable sum in respect of any damage to the premises or neighbouring premises belonging to it, and for expenses incurred in connection with the licence/consent;

e) If the landlord does so and there is a dispute over whether the sum demanded is reasonable, either party may apply to the court to determine the issue. The court can both determine whether the sum is reasonable and compel the landlord to grant consent on the payment of that sum;

f) The section does not apply to certain agricultural and mining leases[353].

278. Case law suggests that the concept of a 'fine' is a broad one. For example, in *Barclays Bank v Daejan Investments (Grove Hall) Ltd*[354], the court held that a condition of consent that the tenant agree to a new break clause amounted to the taking of fine for the purposes of s19(3). The court considered that the words *"or sum of money in the nature of a fine"* was *"merely illustrative"* of what may amount to a fine, and that the concept of a 'fine' encompassed *"any consideration"*. The court concluded that the landlord would not

[352] See *F. W. Woolworth and Company Ltd v Lambert* [1937] Ch 37 at 58-59.

[353] See s19(4).

[354] [1995] 1 EGLR 68.

exercise the break unless it was financially advantageous to do so and so amounted to the taking of a fine.[355]

279. In the context of s144 of the Law of Property Act 1925, which likewise prohibits taking of fines, a condition that for the remainder of the lease term a free public house instead be a tied public house was held to amount to a fine.[356]

Reasonableness and user covenants

280. Unlike alienation and alteration covenants[357], s19(3) of the Landlord and Tenant Act does not upgrade partially qualified covenants into fully qualified covenants[358]. The circumstances in which a landlord may lawfully refuse consent under absolute, partially qualified and fully qualified covenants are discussed in chapter 6.

Breaches and remedies

281. Where under a fully qualified covenant a tenant considers that their landlord has unreasonably refused consent to a change in the user, their options include:

   a) Seeking a declaration from the court that consent has been unreasonably withheld[359]; or

---

[355] 69-70.

[356] *Gardner v Cone* [1928] Ch 955.

[357] So far as the alteration covenant relates to improvements.

[358] *Guardian Assurance Co v Gants Hill Holdings* [1983] EGLR 36.

[359] The County Court has jurisdiction to hear such a claim: s53 of the Landlord and Tenant Act 1954.

b) Proceeding with the change of user without consent. If the tenant is correct that consent has been unreasonably withheld, to do so will not be a breach of the lease[360].

282. Both of these possibilities, and the underlying case law, are discussed in chapter 8. Seeking a declaration from the court, prior to changing the user, is ordinarily the safer if slower option.

283. A tenant has the same options when, under a partially qualified covenant, it considers that the impermissibly landlord has demanded a fine as a condition of consent. If correct, the tenant may proceed to change the user without consent and do so will not breach the covenant.[361] The safer, if slower, option is to seek a determination that a fine has been demanded.[362]

User clauses and the Competition Act 1998

284. User clauses are one means by which a business could restrict competition from operating within its area. Although this is more likely to be achieved with freehold covenants, as the land can be burdened without the need for a landlord and tenant relationship, competition law is also appliable in the leasehold context. The workings of competition law are outside the scope of this work – what follows is by way of summary in order to assist the reader with spotting potential competition law issues.

285. Since 6 April 2011[363], the requirements of the Competition Act 1998 have applied to 'land agreements', which includes leases[364].

---

[360] *Treloar v Bigge* (1874) LR 9 Ex 151. This case and the line of case law which follows it is considered in chapter 8.

[361] See *Barclays Bank Plc v Daejan Investments* [1995] EGLR 68 at 68-70.

[362] As above, s19(3) expressly envisages such claims.

[363] As a result of amendments made by article 2 of the Competition Act 1998 (Land Agreements Exclusion Revocation) Order 2010.

[364] This was common ground in *Martin Retail Group Ltd v Crawley Borough Council* [2014] L & TR 17 at paragraph 19.

By s2 of the Competition Act 1998, agreements between undertakings[365] which (1) may affect trade within the United Kingdom and (2) have as their object or effect the prevention, restriction or distortion of competition within the United Kingdom, are prohibited unless exempt in accordance with the provision of Part 1 of the Act. This is known as the 'Chapter 1 prohibition'. Although not free from doubt, it is likely that that Chapter 1 prohibition only applies to agreements which prevent, restrict or distort competition to an appreciable extent.[366]

286. Any restriction which infringes the Chapter I prohibition is void and unenforceable.

287. Section 9 specifies which agreements are exempt from the Chapter 1 prohibition. An agreement which would otherwise violate the Chapter 1 prohibition is exempt if it:

a) Contributes to improving production or distribution, or to promoting technical or economic progress;

b) Allows consumers a fair share of the resulting benefits;

c) Does not impose restrictions beyond those indispensable to achieving those objectives;

---

365 Which does not include individuals who are not acting as a business.

366 That is the view taken in the guidance – see the OFT guidance *'Land Agreements. The application of competition law following the revocation of the Land Agreements Exclusion Order" of March 2011'* at paragraphs 1.6 and 2.11-2.17. See too *P&S Amusements Ltd v Valley House Leisure Ltd* [2006] EWHC 1510 (Ch) paragraph 22 and *Pirtek (UK) v Joinplace* [2010] EWHC 1641 (Ch) at paragraphs 61-62 although neither sought to authoritatively decide the point, cf. *Aberdeen Journals v Director General of Fair Trading* [2003] CAT 11 at paragraphs 459–460.

d) Does not afford the parties the possibility of eliminating competition in respect of a substantial part of the products in question.

288. The workings on that section, in the context of user clauses in leases, were helpfully considered by the County Court in *Martin Retail Group Ltd v Crawley Borough Council*[367].

289. Helpful guidance on the application of the Chapter 1 prohibition to leases was issued by the Office of Fair Trading in: *'Land Agreements. The application of competition law following the revocation of the Land Agreements Exclusion Order" of March 2011'.* That guidance has since been adopted by the Competition and Markets Authority. That guidance recognises that there are many legitimate reasons why restrictions may be imposed on how land is used and envisages that only a 'minority' of restrictions will infringe competition law.[368]

290. User covenants in leases are considered at paragraphs 4.11-4.12 and 4.30-4.31 of the guidance, which notes that in most cases such covenants are unlikely to restrict competition. Examples given of where there is the potential for an appreciable effect on competition include:

a) Where the landlord is active in a market and seeks, by a user restriction in a land agreement, to limit the availability of land for its downstream competitors – such as where the landlord operates a number of convenience stores in an area and inserts user covenants into its leases prohibiting convenience store use. Determining whether this might appreciably effect competition would involve consideration of whether the landlord possesses 'market power', assessed by

---

367 [2014] L. & T.R. 17.

368 OFT guidance *'Land Agreements. The application of competition law following the revocation of the Land Agreements Exclusion Order" of March 2011'* at paragraph 1.5.

reference to factors such as whether the landlord has the ability to maintain prices above competitive levels, whether there is sufficient competition in the market and whether there is other suitable land available for use by competitors;

b) Exclusivity agreements – for example where a landlord of a shopping centre leases land to a party and agrees not to allow a competitor of the tenant to operate on any other land owned by the landlord.

Summary

291. The principles can be summarised as follows:

a) The uses to which premises may be put are governed not only by the terms of the lease but also by planning law. It is no defence to a breach of planning control that the use is permitted under a tenant's lease;

b) In general, the common law will not imply a term into a lease that the demised premises are fit for any particular use or can be lawfully put to any particular use. The general principle is 'caveat lessee': the tenant takes the premises as they find them;

c) For qualified covenants, s19(3) of the Landlord and Tenant Act 1927 prohibits the taking of a fine as a condition of granting consent to a change of user. Section 19(3) does not apply where the change of user involves any structural alteration to the demised premises;

d) Under s19(3), the landlord may require payment of a reasonable sum in respect of any damage to the premises or neighbouring premises belonging to it, and for expenses incurred in connection with the licence/consent;

e) Since 6 April 2011, the requirements of the Competition Act 1998 have applied to 'land agreements', which includes leases. An anti-competitive user clause with an appreciable effect on competition could, unless exempt, potentially breach the Chapter 1 prohibition in the 1998 Act.

CHAPTER SIX

WHEN IS CONSENT UNLAWFULLY WITHHELD?

Need to distinguish between different types of covenant

292. Tenant covenants can be usefully split into three categories:

a) Absolute covenants, which are expressed as an absolute prohibition and contain no reference to landlord consent (e.g. 'the tenant covenants not to make any alterations to the demised premises');

b) Partially qualified covenants, which prohibit an act without the landlord's consent (e.g. 'the tenant covenants not to make any alterations to the demised premises without the prior written consent of the landlord');

c) Fully qualified covenants, which prohibit an act without the landlord's consent, such consent not to be unreasonably withheld (e.g., 'the tenant covenants not to make any alterations to the demised premises without the prior written consent of the landlord, such consent not to be unreasonably withheld').

293. Subject to the statutory interventions discussed in the preceding chapters, it is a matter for the parties what limitations to place upon a landlord's ability to refuse consent to the act in question. Parties can, if they choose, go further in restricting the landlord's latitude to refuse than is provided for by statute. For example, a clause that the tenant shall not underlet without the consent of the landlord, such consent not to be refused in the case of a reputable sub-tenant would, in the case of such a sub-tenant, leave the landlord no

discretion at all to refuse consent, even if it were reasonable to do so.

Refusal under an absolute covenant

294. An absolute covenant prohibits the specified act absolutely, rather than save in specified circumstances or subject to conditions. Where there is an absolute covenant, the landlord remains free if it wishes to waive the covenant for specific instances but is under no legal obligation to do so. The landlord is not required to behave reasonably in deciding whether or not the waive the prohibition, nor to given reasons if it decides not to do so.

295. The ability of the landlord to waive the covenant does not mean that absolute covenants are, in substance, partially qualified covenants (i.e. that in substance they are restrictions not to do the prohibited act without consent). As recognised by Court of Appeal in *F. W. Woolworth and Company Ltd v Lambert*[369] in the context of s19(1) of the Landlord and Tenant Act 1927, "*...although of course it is true that every covenant can be released by the landlord if he so thinks fit*" the "*the difference between an absolute covenant not to assign and a covenant not to assign without the licence or consent of the landlord*" is "*well recognised*"[370].

296. It will be an unusual case where a tenant has a remedy against their landlord for declining to waive the requirements of an absolute covenant.

Refusal under a partially qualified covenant

297. Partially qualified covenants are, in certain cases, upgraded in the fully qualified covenants by statute. Section 19(1) of the Landlord and Tenant Act 1927 upgrades partially qualified covenants against

---

[369] [1937] Ch 37.

[370] See 58-59.

alienation. Section 19(2) has the same effect for partially qualified covenants against improvements.

298. Outside of those cases, the difficult question arises what limits, if any, there are upon a landlord's ability to refuse consent under a partially qualified covenant. If there are no restrictions at all, then in those cases where there is no statutory upgrade into a fully qualified covenant, there would be no meaningful distinction between an absolute and a partially qualified covenant. Equally, if the landlord is required to act reasonably, then the distinction between a partially qualified and a fully qualified covenant is lost.

299. The answer, it is suggested, lies in fact that under a partially qualified covenant the landlord is, in deciding whether to grant or refuse consent, exercising a contractual discretion in respect of which the law imposes certain duties. In contrast, a landlord deciding whether or not to waive the protection of an absolute covenant is not exercising a discretion within the contract itself and so no additional duties apply.

Duties imposed upon a party exercising discretion under a contract

300. The courts have on a number of occasions in recent years considered the question of what limits, if any, apply where one party to a contract has a discretion which is open to abuse. In *Socimer International Bank Ltd (in liquidation) v Standard Bank London Ltd (No. 2)*[371], Rix LJ put the issue this way:

> *"When a contract allocates only to one party a power to make decisions under the contract which may have an effect on both parties, at least two questions arise. One is, what if any are the limitations on the decision-maker's freedom of decision?"*[372]

[371] [2008] EWCA Civ 116; [2008] Bus L.R. 1304.

[372] Paragraph 60.

301. Reviewing the authorities, Rix LJ answered that question as follows:

> *"It is plain from these authorities that a decision-maker's discretion will be limited, as a matter of necessary implication, by concepts of honesty, good faith, and genuineness, and the need for the absence of arbitrariness, capriciousness, perversity and irrationality. The concern is that the discretion should not be abused. Reasonableness and unreasonableness are also concepts deployed in this context, but only in a sense analogous to Wednesbury unreasonableness..."*[373]

302. *Wednesbury* unreasonableness[374], which was developed in public law as a limiting principle to the discretion of public bodies, has two limbs[375]:

    a) A procedural limb that the requires the decision maker to have had regard to all relevant matters[376] and to disregard any irrelevant matters[377]; and

    b) A substantive limb that the resulting decision is not so unreasonable that no reasonable decision maker could ever have come to it[378].

---

373 Paragraph 66.

374 Which derives from the decision of the Court of Appeal in *Associated Provincial Picture Houses Limited* v *Wednesbury Corporation* [1948] 1 KB 223, [1947] 2 All ER 680, as later explained in *Council of Civil Service Unions v Minister for the Civil Service* [1985] AC 374, [1984] 3 WLR 1174; [1984] 3 All ER 935.

375 As explained in *Braganza v BP Shopping Ltd* [2015] UKSC 17; [2015] 1 WLR 1661 at paragraph 24.

376 See *Braganza v BP Shopping Ltd* [2015] UKSC 17; [2015] 1 WLR 1661 paragraph 29.

377 *Associated Provincial Picture Houses Limited* v *Wednesbury Corporation* [1948] 1 KB 223 at 228.

378 *Council of Civil Service Unions v Minister for the Civil Service* [1985] AC 374 at 410.

303. Importantly, the *Wednesbury* standard is in substance a rationality review only - the court's review of that decision does not permit the court to step into the shoes of the decision maker and decide upon the objective reasonableness of the decision for itself. The distinction was explained further by Lord Sumption JSC in *Hayes v Willoughby*[379] where he explained that:

"Rationality is not the same as reasonableness. Reasonableness is an external, objective standard applied to the outcome of a person's thoughts or intentions... A test of rationality, by comparison, applies a minimum objective standard to the relevant person's mental processes. It imports a requirement of good faith, a requirement that there should be some logical connection between the evidence and the ostensible reasons for the decision, and (which will usually amount to the same thing) an absence of arbitrariness, of capriciousness or of reasoning so outrageous in its defiance of logic as to be perverse."[380]

304. The Supreme Court returned to the issue of contractual discretion in *Braganza v BP Shopping Ltd*[381]. In that case, Baroness Hale was of the view that, where a party to a contract *"is charged with making decisions which affect the rights of both parties to the contract"* and has a clear conflict of interest, a term will be implied to regulate the manner in which the power will be exercised.[382] The court will usually imply a term that *"the decision is made rationally (as well as in good faith) and consistently with its contractual purpose."*[383] Rationality, in this context, meant rational in the *Wednesbury* sense.

305. One issue for the Supreme Court was whether both limbs of the Wednesbury test were applicable, or only the procedural limb. Baroness Hale held that both limbs of the *Wednesbury* test would

---

379 [2013] UKSC 17; [2013] 1 WLR 935.

380 Paragraph 14.

381 [2015] UKSC 17; [2015] 1 WLR 1661.

382 Paragraph 18.

383 Paragraph 30.

apply[384]. Baroness Hale did, however, emphasise that *"whatever term may be implied will depend on the terms and the context of the particular contract involved"*[385] and it was not necessary to reach a 'final conclusion' on the precise extent to which an implied contractual term may differ from the principles applicable to the judicial review of administrative action. Further, it was felt that given that *"the question may arise in so many different contractual contexts, it may well be that no precise answer can be given."*[386]

306. Lord Neuberger, after referring approvingly to the comments of Rix LJ set out above, took substantially the same approach as Baroness Hale.[387] Lord Hodge agreed, including that both limbs of the Wednesbury standard applied, explaining that he thought it was:

"...difficult to treat as rational the product of a process of reasoning if that process is flawed by the taking into consideration of an irrelevant matter or the failure to consider a relevant matter. While the courts have not as yet spoken with one voice, I agree that, in reviewing at least some contractual discretionary decisions, the court should address both limbs of Lord Greene MR's test in Associated Provincial Picture Houses Ltd v Wednesbury Corpn [1948] 1 KB 223, 233–234."[388]

307. Subsequent caselaw has confirmed that a *Braganza* type term will not be implied where one party merely has a contractual power to do something, rather than a contractual discretion to make decisions under the contract.[389] In other words, it is not enough that one party simply has a decision whether or not to exercise a contractual right, a discretion must be involved which entails

---

[384] Paragraph 30.

[385] Paragraph 31.

[386] Paragraph 32.

[387] Paragraph 103.

[388] Paragraph 53.

[389] See for example the discussion in *Shurbanova v Forex Capital Markets Limited* [2017] EWHC 2133 (QB) at paragraphs 91-101.

making an assessment or choosing from a range of options, taking into account the interests of both parties. In such a case, the law will imply a term that the discretion is not to be exercised in an arbitrary, capricious or irrational manner.

Application of the Braganza duty to partially qualified covenants

308. The extent to which a 'Braganza' type duty can be implied into a partially modified covenant, and if so what the content of the duty is, was considered by the Court of Appeal in *Victory Place Management v Kuehn*[390]. In that case, the tenant's lease included a covenant that no animal was to be kept in the flat without consent (i.e. a partially qualified covenant). The landlord of the block of flats had a policy that pets would not be permitted save in special circumstances. The issue arose whether the landlord's discretion was subject to a *Braganza* duty and, if so, whether both limbs of the *Wednesbury* standard applied. The Chancellor:

a) Cautioned that *"public law and private law concepts"* should not be confused and the fact that *"a concept borrowed from public law may inform the kind of term that may be implied in a private law context should not blur the distinction"*[391];

b) Found that it was not necessary to determine whether both limbs of the *Wednesbury* test applied but, obiter, observe that his *"inclination would have been to hold, had it mattered, that both the "process" limb of the Wednesbury test and the "outcome" limb would have been applicable"*[392];

[390] [2018] EWHC 132 (Ch); [2018] HLR 26.

[391] Paragraph 30.

[392] Paragraph 33.

c) Held that, in the context of the case before the court, the requirement for a reasonable process and a rational outcome were *"not high thresholds to meet"*[393];

d) Found that the landlord's policy of 'no pets save in special circumstances' was consistent with the covenant and did not amount to an impermissible pre-determination of applications for consent[394].

309. The above cases support landlords, when considering an application for consent under a partially qualified covenant, as being under an implied obligation to act in good faith and rationally (with both limbs of the *Wednesbury* test applying). The matter is not, however, free from doubt as this conclusion does blur the distinction between partially qualified and fully qualified covenants. It may be revisited by the courts in the future. It should also be borne in mind that the threshold imposed by the *Wednesbury* test is a low one which will often be easy to meet.

Burden of proof

310. Where the tenant succeeds in arguing that a landlord is under a *Braganza* type duty, the burden will lie upon the tenant to prove that the landlord has acted contrary to that duty.[395]

Refusal under a fully qualified covenant

311. The law is more certain where covenants are fully qualified. The circumstances in which the law upgrades a partially qualified covenant into a fully qualified covenant has been explained in the preceding chapters.

---

[393] Paragraph 33.

[394] Paragraph 40.

[395] This being the position at common law – see *International Drilling Fluids Ltd v Louisville Investments (Uxbridge) Ltd* [1986] Ch 513 at 520.

Refusal under fully qualified alienation covenants

312. Section 144 of the Law of Property Act 1925 prohibits the landlord from taking a fine as a condition of consent unless the lease contains an express provision to the contrary.[396]

313. More broadly, in *International Drilling Fluids Ltd v Louisville Investments (Uxbridge) Ltd*[397], Balcombe LJ identified the following principles from the case law for ascertaining whether consent has been unreasonably withheld under a fully qualified alienation covenant:

   a) *"The purpose of a covenant against assignment without the consent of the landlord, such consent not to be unreasonably withheld, is to protect the lessor from having his premises used or occupied in an undesirable way, or by an undesirable tenant or assignee"*;

   b) As a corollary to that first proposition, a landlord is not entitled to refuse his consent to an assignment on grounds which have nothing whatever to do with the relationship of landlord and tenant in regard to the subject matter of the lease. A landlord may not refuse consent where the refusal is designed to achieve a collateral purpose unconnected with the terms of the lease;

   c) The onus of proving that consent has been unreasonably withheld is on the tenant. [Note that for alienation covenants, the burden of proof has since been reversed by s1(6) of the Landlord and Tenant Act 1988 and rests with the landlord];

   d) It is not necessary for the landlord to prove that the conclusions which led him to refuse consent were justified, if

[396] See the discussion in chapter 4.

[397] [1986] Ch 513 at 519-521.

they were conclusions which might be reached by a reasonable man in the circumstances;

e) It may be reasonable for the landlord to refuse his consent to an assignment on the ground of the purpose for which the proposed assignee intends to use the premises, even though that purpose is not forbidden by the lease;

f) Usually, a landlord needs only consider his own relevant interests, but there may be cases *"where there is such a disproportion between the benefit to the landlord and the detriment to the tenant if the landlord withholds his consent to an assignment that it is unreasonable for the landlord to refuse consent"*;

g) Subject to the propositions set out above, it is in each case a question of fact, depending upon all the circumstances, whether the landlord's consent to an assignment is being unreasonably withheld.

314. A significant reform made after the decision in *International Drilling Fluids Ltd v Louisville Investments (Uxbridge) Ltd* was the enactment of the Landlord and Tenant Act 1988, which imposed a series of statutory duties upon landlords in respect of applications for consent to assign, underlet, charge or part with possession of premises.[398] This is a departure from other statutory interventions in this area which have tended to vary tenancies by the implication of a term.[399]

---

398 The duties are set out in chapter 4.

399 For the 1988 Act duties, the tenancy itself remains unaltered - see *No 1 West India Quay (Residential) Ltd v East Tower Apartments Ltd* [2018] EWCA Civ 250; [2018] 1 W.L.R. 5682 at paragraph 21.

315. The Court of Appeal has considered the duties imposed by the Landlord and Tenant 1988 Act on several occasions[400]. It is now established that, under the 1988 Act:

a) Decisions on applications for consent must be given within a reasonable time. A reasonable time is likely to be measured in weeks, not months[401];

b) Whether a landlord's decision to withhold consent to a proposed assignment is reasonable can only be decided by reference to the circumstances existing and known to the landlord at the time the decision to withhold the consent is made[402];

c) It is not necessary for a landlord to prove that the conclusions which led them to refuse consent were justified, if they were conclusions which might be reached by a reasonable person in the circumstances[403];

d) It is only if no reasonable landlord could have withheld consent for the reasons stated by the landlord that a decision to withhold consent will be held to be unreasonable; the court is not entitled to substitute its own view for that of the landlord[404];

---

400 See *Kened Ltd v Connie Investments Limited* (1995) 70 P & CR 370; *Dong Bang Minerva (UK) Ltd v Davina Ltd* (1997) 73 P & CR 253; *Go West Ltd v Spigarolo* [2003] EWCA Civ 17; [2003] QB 1140; *No 1 West India Quay (Residential) Ltd v East Tower Apartments Ltd* [2018] EWCA Civ 250; [2018] 1 W.L.R. 5682.

401 *Go West Ltd v Spigarolo* [2003] EWCA Civ 17; [2003] QB 1140 paragraph 73.

402 *Kened Ltd v Connie Investments Limited* (1995) 70 P & CR 370 at 373.

403 *Kened Ltd v Connie Investments Limited* (1995) 70 P & CR 370 at 374.

404 *Kened Ltd v Connie Investments Limited* (1995) 70 P & CR 370 at 374.

e) A landlord can only rely upon those reasons for refusing consent which were given to the tenant within a reasonable time in writing as required by s1(3). The landlord may not, thereafter, seek to supplement their reasons[405];

f) Where multiple reasons are given for refusing consent, a 'bad' reason will not vitiate a reasonable ground for refusal provided the 'good' ground is freestanding and had an independent causative effect[406];

g) Giving consent subject to conditions that are not reasonable will breach the s1(3)(a) duty to given consent except where it is reasonable to withhold consent[407];

h) It is reasonable for a landlord to require the tenant to undertake to meet their reasonable costs of considering the application[408], but a demand that the tenant indemnify the landlord against all its costs incurred in considering the application will not be reasonable[409].

---

405 See *Go West Ltd v Spigarolo* [2003] EWCA Civ 17; [2003] QB 1140 at paragraphs 19 to 22 and *No 1 West India Quay (Residential) Ltd v East Tower Apartments Ltd* [2018] EWCA Civ 250; [2018] 1 W.L.R. 5682 paragraph 28.

406 *No 1 West India Quay (Residential) Ltd v East Tower Apartments Ltd* [2018] EWCA Civ 250; [2018] 1 W.L.R. 5682 at paragraphs 24-31 and 38-41

407 Section 1(4) Landlord and Tenant Act 1988. In *No 1 West India Quay (Residential) Ltd v East Tower Apartments Ltd* [2018] EWCA Civ 250; [2018] 1 W.L.R. 5682, the Court of Appeal declined to decide whether, to comply with the s1(3)(a) duty, *all* of the conditions given must be reasonable – see paragraph 29.

408 This was common ground before the Court of Appeal in *Dong Bang Minerva (UK) Ltd v Davina Ltd* (1997) 73 P & CR 253 at 256.

409 See *Dong Bang Minerva (UK) Ltd v Davina Ltd* (1997) 73 P & CR 253 at 257.

316. In *Ashworth Fraser v Gloucester City Council*[410], Lord Bingham identified the three *"overriding principles"* as being that:

a) A landlord is not entitled to refuse his consent to an assignment on grounds which have nothing whatever to do with the relationship of landlord and tenant. The basis of the refusal must not be something wholly extraneous from the subject matter of the lease;

b) The question whether the landlord's conduct was reasonable or unreasonable will be one of fact to be decided by the tribunal of fact. While past cases are of *"illustrative value"*, past decisions on their particular facts should not be elevated into principles of law;

c) The landlord's obligation is to show that his conduct was reasonable, not that it was right or justifiable.

Refusal under fully qualified alteration covenants

317. Where a lease contains a fully qualified covenant against alterations, or s19(2) of the Landlord and Tenant Act 1927 applies, the principles by which the reasonableness of refusing consent are judged were confirmed by the Court of Appeal in *Iqbal v Thakrar*[411]. The court took the principles in *International Drilling Fluids Ltd v Louisville Investments (Uxbridge) Ltd* as its starting point, amending them to alterations context. The principles are that[412]:

[410] [2001] UKHL 59; [2001] 1 WLR 2180 at paragraphs 2-5.

[411] [2004] EWCA Civ 592; [2004] 3 EGLR 21.

[412] See *Iqbal v Thakrar* [2004] EWCA Civ 592; [2004] 3 EGLR 21 at paragraph 26.

a) The purpose of the consent is to protect the landlord from the tenant effecting alterations and additions which damage the property interests of the landlord;

b) A landlord is not entitled to refuse consent on grounds which have nothing to do with his property interests.;

c) It is for the tenant to show that the landlord has unreasonably withheld his consent to the proposals which the tenant has put forward. Implicit within that is the necessity for the tenant to make sufficiently clear what his proposals are, so that the landlord knows whether he should refuse or give consent to the alterations or additions;

d) It is not necessary for the landlord to prove that the conclusions which led him to refuse consent were justified, if they were conclusions which might be reached by a reasonable landlord in the particular circumstances;

e) It may be reasonable for the landlord to refuse consent to an alteration or addition required to enable a change of use even if the proposed use is not forbidden by the lease. But whether such refusal is reasonable or unreasonable depends on all the circumstances;

f) While a landlord need usually consider only his own interests, there may be cases where it would be disproportionate for a landlord to refuse consent having regard to the effects on himself and on the tenant respectively.

g) Consent cannot be refused on grounds of pecuniary loss alone. The proper course for the landlord to adopt in such circumstances is to ask for a compensatory payment.

h) In each case it is a question of fact depending on all the circumstances whether the landlord, having regard to the actual reasons which impelled him to refuse consent, acted unreasonably.

Refusal under fully qualified user covenants

318. For fully qualified user covenants, it is considered that the approach of the court in *International Drilling Fluids Ltd v Louisville Investments (Uxbridge) Ltd*[413], set out above, will apply with suitable changes made for the context.

319. As set out in chapter 5, where s19(3) of the Landlord and Tenant Act 1927 applies[414], the landlord may not take a fine as a condition of consent.

What reasons can a landlord reply on? Who bears the burden of proof? Do bad reasons vitiate good reasons?

320. Under the LTA 1988, for alienation applications, landlords are under a statutory duty to give reasons and, where consent is refused, bear the burden of proving that the reasons for refusal are reasonable. Outside of the LTA 1988, which is limited to alienation covenants, the common law principles remain applicable.

321. At common law, a landlord is under no duty to give reasons for refusing an application for consent[415]. However, where no reasons are given, the burden of proving that consent has been reasonably withheld may in substance shift to the landlord[416]. The standard

[413] [1986] Ch 513 at 519-521.

[414] I.e. Where there is a covenant against changing the user without licence or consent and the tenant seeks consent for an alteration of the user which does not involve any structural alteration of the premises.

[415] See *Young v Ashley Gardens Properties* [1903] 2 Ch 112; *Goldstein v Sanders* [1915] 1 Ch 549 at 553.

[416] In *Lambert v FW Woolworth & Co (No. 2)* [1938] Ch 883 at 906, Slesser LJ observed that in his view *"...the onus of proving that the withholding is unreasonable is on the tenant, but if the landlord gives no reason but merely refuses, that, in itself, I think, puts upon him the duty of showing that his action was reasonable."* In *Frederick Berry Ltd v Royal Bank of Scotland* [1949] 1 KB 619. Lord Goddard CJ at 623 held that by those comments Slesser LJ meant

position is that the onus of showing that consent has been unreasonably withheld is upon the tenant.[417]

322. At common law, where a landlord's refusal of consent is challenged, in defending the refusal the landlord is not confined to the reasons previously given to the tenant and the court may take into account any reasons advanced at the hearing[418]. However, the landlord may still only rely upon reasons which actually influenced it at the relevant time, not mere afterthoughts[419].

323. Both under the LTA 1988 and at common law, where multiple reasons are given for refusing consent, some of which are valid grounds for refusal and some of which are unreasonable, the decision to refuse consent will be lawful providing[420]:

a) The good reason is independent of, and not infected by, the bad reason(s); and

b) The landlord would have reached the same decision if no regard had been had to the bad reason(s).

---

no more than that *"if the landlord gives no reason the court would more readily imply that the withholding was unreasonable."*

417 See *International Drilling Fluids Ltd v Louisville Investments (Uxbridge) Ltd* [1986] Ch 513 at 520.

418 *Lovelock v Margo* [1963] 2 QB 786 at 789-790; *Welch v Birrane* (1974) 29 P & CR 102 at 107. In *Welch*, Lawson J considered this to be right in principle where *"the law does not require a landlord to give any reasons at all"*.

419 *Bromley Park Gardens Estates Ltd v Moss* [1982] 1 WLR 1019 at 1033-1034. Where the tenant goes ahead and assigns, believing consent was unreasonably withheld, the relevant date is likely the date of assignment. Where the tenant, without assigning, challenges the refusal in court, it is likely to be the date of refusal. See too *Iqbal v Thakrar* [2004] EWCA Civ 592; [2004] 3 EGLR 21 at paragraph 27.

420 *No 1 West India Quay (Residential) Ltd v East Tower Apartments Ltd* [2018] 1 WLR 5682 at paragraphs 23-27, 31 and 38-41.

Reliance on unreasonable conditions

324. The giving of consent subject to conditions which are reasonable amounts to an unreasonable withholding of consent.[421] It would seem to follow from the case law on bad reasons for refusing consent not vitiating good reasons that the same is true of unreasonable conditions not vitiating a refusal where the landlord would, without regard to those unreasonable conditions, have refused consent due to the tenant's refusal to meet reasonable conditions.

325. Whether this is also the position under the LTA 1988 is a point of uncertainty: the Court of Appeal declined to resolve that question in *No 1 West India Quay (Residential) Ltd v East Tower Apartments Ltd*[422].

Summary

326. In summary:

a) An absolute covenant prohibits the specified act absolutely, rather than save in specified circumstances or subject to conditions. Where there is an absolute covenant, the landlord remains free if it wishes to waive the covenant for specific instances but is under no legal obligation to do so. The landlord is not required to behave reasonably in deciding whether or not the waive the prohibition, nor to give reasons if it decides not to do so;

b) Partially qualified covenants are, in certain cases, upgraded into fully qualified covenants by statute. Section 19(1) of the Landlord and Tenant Act 1927 upgrades partially qualified

---

[421] *No 1 West India Quay (Residential) Ltd v East Tower Apartments Ltd* [2018] 1 WLR 5682.

[422] *No 1 West India Quay (Residential) Ltd v East Tower Apartments Ltd* [2018] 1 WLR 5682 paragraph 29.

covenants against alienation. Section 19(2) has the same effect for partially qualified covenants against improvements;

c) It is arguable that a landlord determining an application under a partially qualified covenant must decide the application rationally and in good faith. Although the precise content of this duty is uncertain and may vary from case to case, the rationality of the landlord's decision making process and ultimate decision are likely to be assessed against the *Wednesbury* standard – these are not high thresholds for the landlord to meet;

d) For fully qualified covenants the principles for assessing the reasonableness of a landlord's refusal of consent are that:

   i. A landlord is not entitled to refuse consent on grounds which have nothing to do with their property interests, nor to achieve a collateral purpose unconnected with the terms of the lease;

   ii. The onus of proving that consent has been unreasonably withheld is on the tenant;

   iii. It is not necessary for the landlord to prove that the conclusions which led them to refuse consent were justified, if they were conclusions which might be reached by a reasonable landlord in the circumstances;

   iv. Usually, a landlord needs only consider their own relevant interests, but there may be cases where there is such a disproportion between the benefit to the landlord and the detriment to the tenant if the landlord withholds consent that it is unreasonable for the landlord to do so;

   v. It is otherwise a question of fact, depending upon all the circumstances, whether the landlord's refusal of consent is unreasonable;

vi. Consent should not ordinarily be refused on grounds of pecuniary loss alone. The proper course for the landlord to adopt in such circumstances is to ask for a compensatory payment;

e) At common law, where a landlord's refusal of consent is challenged, in defending the refusal the landlord is not confined to the reasons previously given to the tenant and the court may take into account additional reasons advanced by the landlord, provided that they are reasons which actually influenced the landlord at the relevant time;

f) Where the duties imposed by the Landlord and Tenant Act 1988 apply:

i. The landlord must decide applications for consent within a reasonable time;

ii. A landlord can only rely upon those reasons for refusing consent which were given to the tenant within a reasonable time, in writing, as required by s1(3);

iii. It is not necessary for a landlord to prove that the conclusions which led them to refuse consent were justified, if they were conclusions which might be reached by a reasonable landlord in the circumstances;

iv. Giving consent subject to conditions that are not reasonable will breach the s1(3)(a) duty to give consent except where it is reasonable to withhold consent;

v. It is reasonable for a landlord to require the tenant to undertake to meet their reasonable costs of considering the application;

g) Both under the Landlord and Tenant Act 1988 and at common law, where multiple reasons are given for refusing consent, some of which are valid grounds for refusal and some of which are unreasonable, the decision to refuse consent will be lawful providing:

    i. The good reason is independent of, and not infected by, the bad reason(s); and

    ii. The landlord would have reached the same decision if no regard had been had to the bad reason(s).

CHAPTER SEVEN

INTERACTION BETWEEN THE LANDLORD AND TENANT ACT 1954 AND ALTERATION, ALIENATION AND USER COVENANTS

327. Many commercial tenants benefit from security of tenure under Part II of the Landlord and Tenant Act 1954, although it is possible to contract out of that security by following the procedure specified in s38A.[423]

328. The 1954 Act is a technical piece of legislation and is the subject of much case law. The discussion which follows is restricted to the issues that can arise concerning alienation, alteration and user covenants.[424]

Adding / removing / amending a covenant in lease renewal proceedings

329. When a tenant with security of tenure under the 1954 Act seeks a new tenancy from the court, the terms of the new tenancy will be determined in accordance with sections 33 to 35 of the 1954 Act[425].

---

[423] Any agreement to exclude the tenant's right to request a new tenancy under the Act which is not reached in accordance with the s38A procedure is void: s38.

[424] For a broader account of the legislation, reference should be made to specialist works on the 1954 Act.

[425] Unless the landlord opposes the grant of a new tenancy and is able to establish one of the s30 grounds of opposition, in which case the application for a new tenancy will fail.

Section 33 governs the duration of the new tenancy[426], s34 governs the rent[427] and s35 governs the other terms of the new tenancy.

330. By s35(1), the other terms of the tenancy shall be *"...such as may be agreed between the landlord and the tenant or as, in default of such agreement, may be determined by the court; and in determining those terms the court shall have regard to the terms of the current tenancy and to all relevant circumstances."*[428]

331. In renewal proceedings, the landlord may seek to amend the terms of the pre-existing lease by adding additional restrictions upon the permitted user, or the tenant's ability to alter the premises or dispose of them. Equally, in renewal proceedings, the tenant may seek to liberalise the existing restrictions. The opposite can also be the case because a lease with less onerous tenant covenants will usually attract a higher rent on the open market from a willing lessor. A landlord wishing to maximise the rent of the new tenancy may then seek to liberalise the covenants in the new lease and a tenant seeking to minimise the rent may seek to make them more onerous.

332. The leading authority on the correct approach to the court's s35 discretion is the decision of the House of Lords in *O'May v City of London Real Property Co. Ltd*[429]. In that case, it was held that:

---

[426] Which shall be, in the default of agreement, *"such a tenancy as may be determined by the court to be reasonable in all the circumstances"* up to a maximum of 15 years.

[427] Which shall be, in the default of agreement, the rent at which the holding might reasonably be expected to be let in the open market by a willing lessor, disregarding certain matters (such as tenant goodwill and certain tenant improvements).

[428] Section 35(2) confirms that 'all the relevant circumstances' include *"the operation of the provisions of the Landlord and Tenant (Covenants) Act 1995."*

[429] [1983] 2 A.C. 726.

a) In *"having regard to the terms of the current tenancy and to all relevant circumstances"* under s.35(1) the court must begin by considering the terms of the current tenancy[430];

b) Those terms are the starting point and the burden of persuading the court to impose a change in those terms against the will of either party must rest on the party proposing the change[431];

c) Any change proposed must, in the circumstances of the case, be fair and reasonable[432], and should take into account, amongst other things:

    i. The comparatively weak negotiating position of a sitting tenant requiring renewal, particularly in conditions of scarcity[433]; and

    ii. The general purpose of the 1954 Act which is to protect the business interests of the tenant so far as they are affected by the approaching termination of the current lease in particular as regards their security of tenure[434]

d) The court will not, however, seek to petrify the terms of the lease and where they are obsolete or deficient the court may change them. As Lord Wilberforce explained, the words 'have regard to' in s35 *"...are elastic: they compel something between an obligation to reproduce existing terms and an unfettered right to substitute others."* The burden is on the party proposing the change to justify it, with *"strong and cogent evidence"*, but, if

430 Pg740E.

431 Pg740F-G and 747F.

432 Pg740F-G.

433 Pg740H.

434 P740H-741A.

such reasons are shown, the court may allow the change and there is:

"...certainly no intention shown to freeze, or in the metaphor used by learned counsel, to "petrify" the terms of the lease. In some cases, especially where the lease is an old one, many of its terms may be out of date, or unsuitable in relation to the new term to be granted."[435]

333. Recent case law tends to emphasise the strength of reasons required to justify a change from the terms of the current tenancy. For example, in *EE Ltd v Stephenson*[436], Fancourt J explained that:

"Section 35 of the 1954 Act operates to limit changes in the terms of the tenancy (other than rent and duration) against the will of either party. This is an aspect of the provision of business continuity for the tenant, although it is sometimes the tenant who seeks the change. A heavy onus lies on the party seeking a change to justify it, in terms of overall fairness: O'May. Changes are readily justified where the law has changed... Changes may be justified where it is fair to both parties..."[437]

334. Those comments were subsequently cited by the Court of Appeal in *On Tower UK Ltd v JH & FW Green Ltd*[438], with Newey LJ adding that, in practice, *"a variation in terms to the prejudice of the tenant may be hard to justify, the general purpose of the 1954 Act being to protect the business interests of tenants."*[439]

335. It follows that the fact a proposed change will greatly benefit one party is unlikely to be a sufficient justification for a change to the

---

[435] Pg747E-H.

[436] [2021] UKUT 167 (LC); [2021] 4 WLR 116.

[437] Paragraph 54.

[438] [2021] EWCA Civ 1858; [2022] 4 WLR 27.

[439] Paragraph 47.

existing terms of a tenancy[440]. While the terms of any alteration, user or alienation clause can be changed from the provision made by the pre-existing lease, strong and cogent evidence will be needed to justify the change, particularly if it would be prejudicial to the security of tenant in their business, which it is the policy of the 1954 Act to protect.[441]

User covenants in lease renewal proceedings

336. There are several reasons why the landlord or the tenant might wish to vary the user covenant in lease renewal proceedings. Making the covenant broader would, for example, be likely to make the lease more easily assignable and achieve a higher rent. Conversely, narrowing a broad user covenant to the use actually being made of the premises by the tenant would allow the landlord a greater degree of control and be likely to result in a lower rent.

Acceptability of narrowing the user clause

337. It is open to the parties in lease renewal proceedings to agree the form of the user clause in the new lease – it is only in default of such agreement that the court will resolve the issue.

338. Where the parties are not in agreement, the court is unlikely to modify a user covenant in such a way as to restrict the tenant carrying on the business which it has actually been conducting from the premises. In *Gold v Brighton Corp.*[442], Parker LJ observed that it was:

---

[440] A point recognised in *Charles Clements (London) Ltd v Rank City Wall* (1978) 246 EG 739.

[441] See *Gold v Brighton Corporation* [1956] 1 WLR 1291: *"Turning now to the Act of 1954, I think it plainly intends to protect the tenant in respect of his business"* (Denning LJ at 1293), *"The Act was designed to provide security for the tenant"* (Birkett LJ at 1295).

[442] [1956] 1 WLR 1291.

"...it is difficult to think of any considerations which would justify changing the restrictions on user in such a way as to alter or limit the nature of the business which the tenant has lawfully carried out on those premises and which it is clearly the object of the Act to preserve."[443]

339. Where a tenant seeks to change the terms of the lease to introduce an extremely restrictive clause with the objective of minimising the rent, that is unlikely to be acceptable. In *Aldwych Club v Copthall Property Co. Ltd*[444], Pennycuick J held that, while under s35 the court has the widest possible discretion, he had:

"...great difficulty in imagining an instance in which the Court could properly exercise its discretion under section 35 by introducing a restriction at the instance of the tenant himself, with the consequence and, indeed, the sole purpose, of bringing about a diminution of the rent to be determined under section 34."

340. In that case, the lease contained a user covenant *"Not to use or allow the demised premises to be used for any purpose other than as a club without the previous consent in writing of the lessors which consent shall not be unreasonably refused."* It was common ground that the landlord could not reasonably refuse consent to use the premises as offices and that the rent in a lease permitting both office and club use was higher than a lease restricted to club use. Rejecting a submission from the tenant that the new lease should *"restrict the use of the premises still further by confining it to use as a club with no exception for any other purpose with the consent of the lessors"*, Pennycuick J held that he could:

"...not see any ground upon which the Court at the instance of the tenant and contrary to the wishes of the landlord could thus sterilise the use of the premises to their present use with the consequences that there would be excluded from the hypothetical open market the class of

---

[443] 1296.

[444] (1962) 185 EG 219.

would-be tenants most likely to pay the best rent, namely, those wishing to use the premises as offices."

Acceptability of broadening the user clause

341. It is likewise unlikely that a court will broaden a user covenant, against the will of the tenant, in order to maximise the rent payable to the landlord. In *Charles Clements (London) Ltd v Rank City Wall*[445], the landlord proposed modifying an existing user covenant against using the premises other than for the business of a retail cutler without consent to add that such consent was not to be unreasonably withheld. The effect would be to increase the number of permissible users and the rent payable. The tenant objected the proposed change. The court held that absent some special reason (not present on the facts) the covenant should not be modified – that the change would be beneficial to the landlord was not of itself sufficient justification. Goulding J held that the language of s35 was *"...a guide to the court that Parliament wanted the terms of the current tenancy to be considered in the forefront in every case, along with any relevant circumstances of the particular case"*, and continued that:

"Here I have no evidence of any special facts affecting the property that are not common to all retail premises in high-class business areas. If the parties are to be at liberty to insist on changes in the terms of the existing tenancy simply because they consider them beneficial to themselves, a field would be opened which I think the court would find it bewildering to traverse. Every tenant could volunteer to accept increased liabilities as to this or that matter for the purpose of getting, on terms that he thought might ultimately profit him, a lower rent; every landlord might press this or that concession on the tenant because it would enable him to say the open market rent was a higher rent. It therefore appears to me, for the purposes of the present case, that the right course is to take the terms of the existing lease as a sufficient guide in this respect, and

[445] (1978) 246 EG 739.

not to make the alteration desired by the landlord since no special reason is shown for it and the tenant objects to it."

342. The court has made much the same point where it is the tenant which seeks an expanded user clause in order to maker the new lease easier to assign. For example, in *Gold v Brighton Corp*, Denning LJ stated that *"It is to be remembered that the object of this Act is to protect the tenant in respect of his or her business, and not to put a new saleable asset into her hands."*[446]

Relationship between the rent payable under the new tenancy and the permitted user in the new tenancy

343. In lease renewals under the 1954 Act the rent payable is the last matter determined by the court, by reference to the terms of the new tenancy. As explained above, the terms of the user clause will obviously have an effect on the market rent a willing lessee would pay.[447]

344. In doing so, the court will examine the user permitted by the lease and, subject to suitable evidence, any other user to which a landlord would be unable to object where the lease makes provision for a change in the user with the landlord's consent, such consent not to be unreasonably withheld.[448]

---

[446] [1956] 1 WLR 1291 at 1294.

[447] In *Aldwych Club v Copthall Property Co. Ltd* (1962) 185 EG 219 the court observed that it was 'obvious' that *"any condition restrictive on user which may be introduced into the tenancy under section 35 must be taken into account in determining the rent under section 34."*

[448] See *Aldwych Club v Copthall Property Co. Ltd* (1962) 185 EG 219, discussed above, where the new rent was calculated taking into account both the club and offices use.

User and breaches of planning control

345. The court will not grant a new lease for a use which is in breach of planning control. For example, in *Turner & Bell v Searles (Stanford-le-Hope) Ltd*[449], the court refused to grant a new lease to a tenant which had been using the premises as a coach depot in breach of planning control and where the tenant accepted that, were a new lease granted, it would continue to do so. Roskill LJ took the view *"most emphatically that where the purpose of a new lease or a tenancy is to enable a business or activities of one kind or another to be carried on obviously contrary to the law it would be quite wrong for the court to close its eyes to that fact."*[450]

<u>Alteration covenants in lease renewal proceedings</u>

346. For the reasons explained above, if in renewal proceedings one of the parties wishes to alter the provision made in the existing lease for alterations, the burden is upon that party to justify the change.

347. By way of an illustration of the sorts of considerations that may be relevant, in *Amarjee v Barrowfen Properties*[451], the pre-existing yearly lease contained no terms other than the rent. On renewal, the tenant wished to be permitted to carry out any alterations subject to the landlord's consent, not to be unreasonably withheld, subject to a provision that he reinstates at the end of the term. The landlord was content with such a term but sought to limit it to non-structural alterations. The court found for the landlord because:

a) The tenant had not adduced any evidence of having plans to structurally alter the building and it was *"not easy to see why he should need to"*; and

449 (1977) 33 P. & C.R. 208.

450 At 212.

451 [1993] 2 EGLR 133.

b) The other lessees in the parade of shops had no right to make structural alterations and the judge could *"see difficulties in permitting one tenant to do something denied to other tenants, including his immediate neighbour, whose premises form part of the same structure."*

Alienation covenants in lease renewal proceedings

348. Given the importance to tenants of the ability to assign, powerful reasons will need to be shown before the court will narrow an existing alienation clause in renewal proceedings.[452] The greater the reduction in the tenant's right to alienate that is proposed, the more powerful the reasons will need to be. In *Cardshops v Davies*[453], the existing lease provided that the tenant would not assign without the previous consent in writing of the lessors, such consent not to be unreasonably withheld. In the renewal proceedings, the landlord sought to amend the alienation clause to add a requirement that, before assigning, the tenant first offer to surrender the lease to the landlord for no consideration. Refusing the make the change, Edmund Davies LJ noted that the proposed term *"imperilled the whole existence of such goodwill as these tenants had built up"* and was *"so novel and burdensome a departure from the terms of the former tenancy as not to be permissible under the Act."*[454]

Landlord and Tenant (Covenants) Act 1995

349. All leases granted pursuant the 1954 Act will now be 'new tenancies' for the purposes of the Landlord and Tenant (Covenants) Act 1995, the workings of which are discussed in chapter 3. Section 35(2) of the 1954 Act confirms that the *"operation of the provisions of the Landlord and Tenant (Covenants) Act 1995"* forms part of 'all

[452] See for example *Cardshops v Davies* [1971] 1 WLR 591 at 596 (Widgery LJ).

[453] [1971] 1 WLR 591 at 596.

[454] At 595.

relevant circumstances' to which the court must have regard in determining the terms of the new lease under s35(1).

350. In renewal proceedings, landlords often seek a term that, as a condition of any assignment, the tenant enter into an authorised guarantee agreement. Case law suggests that the court is likely to limit to landlord's ability to require an authorised guarantee agreement to instances where it is reasonable to do so.[455]

Applicability of the Landlord and Tenant Act 1954 where the use of the premises for a business use is in breach of covenant

351. Part II of the 1954 Act only applies to those tenancies in which *"the property comprised in the tenancy is or includes premises which are occupied by the tenant and are so occupied for the purposes of a business carried on by him or for those and other purposes"*: s23(1). For these purposes, 'business' includes *"a trade, profession or employment and includes any activity carried on by a body of persons, whether corporate or unincorporate"*: s23(2).

352. Section 23(4) of the 1954 Act provides that:

"Subject to subsection (5), where the tenant is carrying on a business, in all or any part of the property comprised in a tenancy, in breach of a prohibition (however expressed) of use for business purposes which subsists under the terms of the tenancy and extends to the whole of that property, this Part of this Act shall not apply to the tenancy unless the immediate landlord or his predecessor in title has consented to the breach or the immediate landlord has acquiesced therein.

In this subsection the reference to a prohibition of use for business purposes does not include a prohibition of use for the purposes of a specified business, or of use for purposes of any but a specified business, but save as aforesaid includes a prohibition of use for the purposes of

[455] See, for example, *Wallis Fashion Group Ltd v CGU Life Assurance Ltd* (2001) 81 P & CR 28 at paragraphs 21 to 29.

some one or more only of the classes of business specified in the definition of that expression in subsection (2) of this section."

353. The effect of s23(4) is, broadly, to take tenancies outside of the 1954 Act where, although they are being used for business purposes, business uses are prohibited by the tenancy. An exception is made where the prohibited use has been consented to or acquiesced in.

354. The effect of the second half of s23(4) is that:

a) A tenancy which contains a covenant 'not to use the premises for business purposes' is outside of the 1954 Act, even if used for such purposes;

b) A tenancy which contains a covenant which, by implication, excludes all business uses, such as to use the premises as a single dwelling house only, is outside of the 1954 Act even if used for such purposes;

c) A tenancy which contains a covenant to use the premises for a specific business use, for example to use the premises as a café only, is within the 1954 Act, even if the tenant is using the property for some other (non-café) business;

d) A tenancy which contains a covenant precluding a specific use, for example not to use the premises as a cafe, is within the 1954 Act even if the tenant is using the premises as a café;

e) A tenancy which contains a covenant not to use the premises for the purposes of any trade, employment, or business activity (but which did not preclude use for a profession), and which was used for the purposes of a trade, would be taken outside the 1954 Act. This is because the covenant is "*a prohibition of use for the purposes of some one or more only of the classes of business specified in the definition of that expression in subsection (2) of this section*", and such a prohibition is included within the types of covenant which when breached take the tenancy outside of the 1954 Act.

355. Special provision is made by s23(5) for 'home business' tenancies[456].

Summary

356. In summary:

a) It is open to the parties in lease renewal proceedings to agree the terms of the new lease. It is only in default of such agreement that the court will do so;

b) For terms other than duration and rent, s35 applies, under which:

   i. The court will begin by considering the terms of the current tenancy. Those terms are the starting point and the burden of persuading the court to impose a charge in those terms against the will of either party must rest on the party proposing the change;

   ii. Any change proposed must, in the circumstances of the case, be fair and reasonable;

   iii. The court will not, however, seek to petrify the terms of the lease and where they are obsolete or deficient the court may change them;

c) The court is unlikely to modify a user covenant in such a way as to restrict the tenant carrying on the business which it has actually been conducting from the premises;

d) Where a tenant seeks to change the terms of the lease to introduce an extremely restrictive clause with the objective of

[456] Defined by s43ZA.

minimising the rent, that is unlikely to be acceptable. That the change would be beneficial to the tenant is not of itself sufficient justification;

e) It is likewise unlikely that a court would broaden a user covenant, against the will of the tenant, in order to maximise the rent payable to the landlord. That the change would be beneficial to the landlord is not of itself sufficient justification;

f) The court will not grant a new lease for a use which is in breach of planning control;

g) Given the importance to tenants of the ability to assign, powerful reasons will need to be shown before the court will narrow an existing alienation clause in renewal proceedings.

CHAPTER EIGHT

REMEDIES FOR BREACH OF COVENANT

357. The aim of this chapter is to bring to the reader's attention issues relating to remedies which commonly arise in respect of alteration, alienation and user covenants in commercial property. For an account of the law of remedies generally, reference should be made to specialist works.

Tenant remedies where a landlord unreasonably refuses consent

358. The issue which will most often confront tenants in the context of alienation, alteration and user covenants is what to do where it is considered that their landlord has unreasonably refused consent under a qualified covenant.

Tenant's ability to proceed in the absence of consent

359. It is well established that, where a landlord unreasonably refuses consent under a fully qualified covenant, the tenant is entitled to proceed with the subject matter of its application (i.e. assign, underlet, alter the premises/user) without the need for consent, and to do so will not amount to a breach of the alteration/alienation/user covenant.

360. *Treloar v Bigge*[457] is often cited as the case which established this rule. There, a lessee covenanted not to assign demised premises without the lessor's consent in writing, such consent not to be arbitrarily withheld. The court held that this did not amount to a covenant by the lessor not to refuse consent arbitrarily. Rather, the words qualified the lessee's obligation, with the consequence that

[457] (1874) LR 9 Ex 151.

where there was an arbitrary refusal the lessee was at liberty to assign without the lessor's consent, without breach of covenant.

361. Kelly CB held that the words 'such consent is not to be arbitrarily withheld:

> *"...do not constitute a covenant on which the lessee can sue, but are words, the only effect of which is to qualify the generality of the phrase into which they are introduced... The words, taken grammatically, do not seem to me to amount to an undertaking by the lessor, but are a part of the same sentence as that containing the lessee's covenant, and qualify its generality. They prevent that covenant operating in any case of arbitrary refusal on the part of the lessor..."*[458]

362. Amphlett B was of the same view, holding that the words ought to:

> *"...be construed as a qualification on the covenant of the lessee. That covenant is in derogation of his common law rights, and it is more convenient and reasonable to hold that the words were introduced to limit the generality of the covenant than to hold them to impose an obligation on the lessor. The true interpretation of the words, I think, is to release the plaintiff from his covenant not to assign without the plaintiff's assent, if that assent is arbitrarily withheld. If that be so they cannot be construed as creating a cross liability. They either qualify the tenant's covenant, or they create a covenant on the landlord's part. They cannot do both..."*[459]

363. So, where this rule applies, the tenant may proceed without consent but will not have any claim for damages against the landlord for an unreasonable refusal of consent.[460]

---

[458] 154-155.

[459] 156.

[460] See *No 1 West India Quay (Residential) Ltd v East Tower Apartments Ltd* [2018] 1 W.L.R. 5682 paragraph 18.

364. While *Treloar v Bigge* concerned an alienation covenant, the rule has since been held to be applicable not just to alienation covenants[461], but also to alteration[462] and user covenants[463].

365. Tenants should think carefully before pursuing this option. It can be high risk because, if the landlord subsequently establishes that the refusal of consent was reasonable, then the tenant will be in breach of covenant. Outside of alienation covenants, to which the statutory duties imposed by the Landlord and Tenant Act 1988 apply, this option can be especially high risk because:

a) The tenant may not know all of the landlord's reasons for withholding consent[464]; and

b) The burden of showing that consent has been unreasonably withheld rests on the tenant.

Proceedings for a declaration that consent has been unreasonably withheld

366. An alternative option open to tenants is to commence legal proceedings and claim a declaration that consent has been unreasonably withheld. It will often be advisable for a tenant to also claim a declaration that it may assign/undertake the improvements etc. without any further application for licence or consent.

367. A claim for declarative relief may be brought in the High Court. The County Court will also have jurisdiction by virtue of s53(1) of the Landlord and Tenant Act 1954, which states that:

---

[461] See for example *West* v. *Gwynne* [1911] 2 Ch 1; *Moat v Martin* [1950] 1 KB 175 at 180; *No 1 West India Quay (Residential) Ltd v East Tower Apartments Ltd* [2018] 1 W.L.R. 5682 paragraph 18.

[462] See *F. W. Woolworth and Company, Limited v Lambert* [1937] Ch 37 at 53.

[463] See *Barclays Bank Plc v Daejan Investments* [1995] EGLR 68 at 68-70.

[464] See the discussion in chapter 6 on landlord reasons.

"(1) Where a landlord withholds his licence or consent—

(a) to an assignment of the tenancy or a subletting, charging or parting with the possession of the demised property or any part thereof, or

(b) to the making of an improvement on the demised property or any part thereof, or

(c) to a change in the use of the demised property or any part thereof, or to the making of a specified use of that property,

and the High Court has jurisdiction to make a declaration that the licence or consent was unreasonably withheld, then without prejudice to the jurisdiction of the High Court the county court shall have the like jurisdiction whatever the net annual value for rating of the demised property is to be taken to be for the purposes of the County Courts Act 1984 and notwithstanding that the tenant does not seek any relief other than the declaration."

Declaration that the landlord has levied a fine contrary to s19(3) of the Landlord and Tenant Act 1927

368. As discussed in chapter 5, s19(3) of the LTA 1927 prohibits a landlord from demanding a fine as a condition of consenting to an alteration of the user of demised premises which does not involve structural alterations. However, a 'reasonable sum' may be demanded in *"respect of any damage to or diminution in the value of the [landlord's] premises or any neighbouring premises"* owned by the landlord, and in respect of any *"legal or other expenses incurred in connection with such licence or consent."*

369. Where there is a dispute over whether a sum demanded by a landlord is reasonable or amounts to a fine, either party may seek a declaration from the court. Such claims are envisaged by s19(3) which continues that *"Where a dispute as to the reasonableness of any such sum has been determined by a court of competent jurisdiction, the*

landlord shall be bound to grant the licence or consent on payment of the sum so determined to be reasonable."

370. It should be noted that, if a landlord seeks a sum from the tenant which is later determined to be reasonable, the court may compel the landlord to grant consent on the payment of that sum.

Claims for damages

371. As set out above, one consequence of the rule in *Treloar v Bigge* is that, at common law, a tenant faced by an unreasonable refusal of consent has no claim in damages.

372. The position was judged to be unsatisfactory by the Law Commission in its report which led to the Landlord and Tenant Act 1988, which imposes a set of statutory duties upon landlords regarding alienation covenants. Where those statutory duties are breached, the tenant may pursue a claim in damages against the landlord[465], provided the tenant can prove that the breach has caused it some loss.[466]

Landlord remedies for tenant breaches of covenant

373. Where a tenant has acted in breach of an alienation, alteration or user covenant, potential remedies open to the landlord include (1) the forfeiture of the lease; (2) a claim for damages and (3) a claim for an injunction.

Forfeiture of the lease

374. Commercial leases almost invariably contain a forfeiture clause which permits, but does require, the landlord to 're-enter the premises' and determine the term in the event of a tenant breach of

---

[465] Section 4 Landlord and Tenant Act 1988.

[466] *No 1 West India Quay (Residential) Ltd v East Tower Apartments Ltd* [2018] 1 WLR 5682 paragraph 22.

covenant. Where there is no such forfeiture clause there is no such right so this should always be checked.

375. There has been significant statutory intervention regulating the circumstances in which a landlord may forfeit a lease, and how forfeiture it to be effected. For breaches of covenant other than the non-payment of rent[467], before a forfeiture clause can be exercised, s146 of the Law of Property Act 1925 requires the landlord to serve a notice on the tenant (a "s146 notice"). Section 146 requires that:

"(1) A right of re-entry or forfeiture under any proviso or stipulation in a lease for a breach of any covenant or condition in the lease shall not be enforceable, by action or otherwise, unless and until the lessor serves on the lessee a notice—

(a) specifying the particular breach complained of; and

(b) if the breach is capable of remedy, requiring the lessee to remedy the breach; and

(c) in any case, requiring the lessee to make compensation in money for the breach;

and the lessee fails, within a reasonable time thereafter, to remedy the breach, if it is capable of remedy, and to make reasonable compensation in money, to the satisfaction of the lessor, for the breach..."

376. Section 146 has effect *"notwithstanding any stipulation to the contrary"* in the lease.[468]

377. By s146, where the breaches are capable of remedy it is therefore a pre-condition of exercising the right to forfeit that, following the service of the s146 notice, the tenant has failed to remedy the breach

[467] Section 146(11) Law of Property Act 1925.

[468] Section 146(12) Law of Property Act 1925.

within a reasonable time and failed to make compensation if such is requested.

Form and content of s146 notices / identifying the breaches of covenant

378. There is no prescribed form for a s146 notice and it is possible to construe a s146 notice out of correspondence, providing the requirements of the section are met[469]. A s146 notice need not actually refer to s146.[470] Nor is a notice invalidated by the failure to demand compensation in money[471]. That said, given the technicalities in this area of the law, it will usually be advisable to make use of a precedent notice from a legal stationer.

379. Where there is some doubt about the validity of a notice already served, a fresh notice may be served without prejudice to the validity of a previous notice (but any such notice should not be served 'without prejudice' generally, as such a notice would be ineffective).

380. To be valid, a s146 notice must:

a) Specify the particular breaches complained of, which must be subsisting, so that the tenant may have an opportunity to remedy them (if capable of remedy) before action is commenced. However, the notice does not have to direct the tenant how to remedy the breaches specified[472];

b) If the breach is capable of remedy, require the lessee to remedy the breach. This is often achieved by use of the words 'remedy the breach, if it is capable of being remedied';

---

[469] *Van Haarlam v Kasner Charitable Trust* (1992) 64 P & CR 214 at 222.

[470] *Van Haarlam v Kasner Charitable Trust* (1992) 64 P & CR 214 at 222.

[471] *Van Haarlam v Kasner Charitable Trust* (1992) 64 P & CR 214 at 222.

[472] Indeed, it will often be better not to do so – how to remedy the breach is a matter for the tenant.

c) Give the tenant a reasonable time to remedy the breach. The time must be reasonable for the tenant to remedy all of the breaches specified in the notice and seek advice on how to proceed. What is 'a reasonable time' is a question of fact in each case. A form of words often used is to require the tenant 'to remedy the breaches within a reasonable time so far as they are capable of remedy'. A forfeiture commenced prior to the expiry of a reasonable time will be invalid.

381. A s146 notice must be served by the landlord to whom the right of re-entry is reserved on the tenant for the time being. If there is doubt as to who the tenant actually is, it is sufficient to address the notice simply to 'the lessee'. Any requirements governing the services of notices in the particular lease should be followed.

When is a breach of covenant remediable?

382. The modern approach to determining whether a breach of covenant is remediable was set out by Staughton LJ in *Savva v Hussein*[473]. After accepting that it was *"established law"* that the breach of a covenant not to assign without consent cannot be remedied[474], Staughton LJ continued that for other cases:

> *"...the question is: whether the remedy referred to is the process of restoring the situation to what it would have been if the covenant had never been broken, or whether it is sufficient that the mischief resulting from a breach of the covenant can be removed. When something has been done without consent, it is not possible to restore the matter wholly to the situation which it was in before the breach. The moving finger writes and cannot be recalled. That is not to my mind what is meant*

[473] (1997) 73 P & CR 150.

[474] Citing the decision of the Court of Appeal in *Scala House & District Property Co. Ltd. v Forbes* [1974] QB 575.

by a remedy, it is a remedy if the mischief caused by the breach can be removed."[475]

383. This is a more flexible approach than was taken in earlier cases. This flexible approach was approved, obiter, by the Supreme Court in *Wickland (Holdings) Ltd v Telchadder*[476]. The situation therefore appears to be as follows:

a) Breaches of alteration covenants will typically be remediable. The question is whether the alterations can in fact be undone[477];

b) Breaches of user covenants will typically be remediable by ceasing the unauthorised use. However, the case law recognises some exceptions – specifically where the nature of the prohibited user is immoral and stigmatises the premises, such as the use of premises for prostitution[478]. The scope of this exception is a matter of some uncertainty given the flexible approach now applied[479];

c) The position for breaches of alienation covenants is somewhat uncertain. On the current state of the case law, a breach of a covenant not to assign is likely irremediable[480].

---

475 (1997) 73 P & CR 150 at 154.

476 [2014] USKC 57; [2014] 1 WLR 4004. See paragraphs 28, 31 and 38.

477 *Savva v Hussein* (1997) 73 P & CR 150 at 154.

478 *Governors of Rugby School v Tannahill* [1935] 1 KB 87. See to the discussion on immoral user in *Patel v K&J Restaurants Ltd* [2010] EWCA Civ 1211; [2011] L & TR 6.

479 See the discussion in *Akici v LR Butlin Ltd* [2005] EWCA Civ 1296; [2006] 1 WLR 201 at paragraph 68.

480 *Scala House & District Property Co. Ltd. v Forbes* [1974] QB 575 at 588E, 591D, 591E; *Savva v Hussein* (1997) 73 P & CR 150 at 154. See too *Akici v LR Butlin Ltd* [2005] EWCA Civ 1296; [2006] 1 WLR 201 at paragraph 67.

By the same reasoning, the breach of a covenant against sub-letting should also be irremediable[481];

d) However, not all breaches of an alienation covenant are incapable of remedy. In *Akici v LR Butlin Ltd*[482], the Court of Appeal held that the sharing of possession or occupation which fell short of creating or transferring a legal interest was capable of remedy[483].

e) The question of whether charging a lease is irremediable is uncertain. In *Akici v LR Butlin Ltd*, the Court of Appeal observed that it probably followed from the cases on assignment and subletting that charging a lease was irremediable, but considered that position as *"arguably unsatisfactory"*[484].

Waiver of right to forfeit

384. The right to forfeit is an option reserved to the landlord – it is up to the landlord whether to take advantage of it or not. The landlord is put to election – and if the landlord elects not to forfeit, the right to forfeit in respect of the breach is waived.

385. A waiver of the right to forfeit will occur where the landlord does acts which are consistent only with treating the lease as continuing

[481] This was the view of Russell LJ in *Scala House & District Property Co. Ltd. v Forbes* [1974] QB 575 – see 588E. See however the doubts about the decision expressed in *Akici v LR Butlin Ltd* [2005] EWCA Civ 1296; [2006] 1 WLR 201 at paragraph 67.

[482] [2005] EWCA Civ 1296; [2006] 1 WLR 201.

[483] *Akici v LR Butlin Ltd* [2005] EWCA Civ 1296; [2006] 1 WLR 201 at paragraphs 73 to 75.

[484] *Akici v LR Butlin Ltd* [2005] EWCA Civ 1296; [2006] 1 WLR 201 at paragraph 67.

(and so are inconsistent with electing to determine it by forfeiture). The essential elements of waiver are:

a) That the landlord has actual knowledge of the basic facts which constitute the relevant breach[485]; and

b) That the landlord[486] acts in a way which is consistent only with the continued existence of the lease. Demanding or accepting rent for periods post-dating the breach are the classic examples of this[487]; and

c) That the landlord communicates the implicit recognition of the continued existence of the lease to the tenant.

386. In *Faiz v Burnley*[488], the Court of Appeal confirmed that:

a) What entitles the landlord to forfeit the lease is a breach of covenant, whether or not he knows that the breach has been committed. If a landlord forfeits a lease, *"it is the breach that he relies on; not the date when he became aware of the breach"*[489];

b) For demands of rent, it does not matter whether the rent accrued due before or after the date of the landlord's *knowledge*, but whether it accrued due before or after the date of the *breach* of which the landlord (now) has knowledge;[490]

---

[485] The knowledge of the landlord's authorised agents may be imputed to the landlord.

[486] Potentially via its authorised agents.

[487] Where rent inadvertently accepted, provided it is repaid as soon as possible, there will not be a waiver of the right to forfeit - see *John Lewis Properties plc v Viscount Chelsea* (1993) 67 P & CR 120, [1993] 2 EGLR 77 at 139-140.

[488] [2021] EWCA Civ 55; [2021] 2 WLR 1115.

[489] Paragraph 26.

[490] Paragraph 28.

c) The critical question is *"whether the date on which the rent fell due preceded or post-dated the breach, rather than the date of the landlord's knowledge, provided that, when he demanded or accepted the rent, the landlord knew that the breach had been committed"*[491];

d) *"...the principle is that waiver takes place where the landlord demands or accepts rent which accrued due after the date of a breach known to the landlord"*. So, where the breach consists of an unlawful sub-letting, to waive the breach, the landlord must *"know not only that the sub-letting has taken place, but also that the rent demanded or accepted accrued due after the date of the breach."*[492]

Continuing v once-and-for-all breaches

387. The law makes a distinction between 'once-and-for-all' breaches of covenant (deemed to take place at a single point in time) and 'continuing' breaches of covenant (for which a new breach of covenant is deemed to occur every day for so long as the breach continues). This matters because, if the right to forfeit for a once-and-for breach is waived, the right is lost forever. If the right to forfeit for a continuing breach of covenant is waived, a fresh breach occurs the next day and there is a new right to forfeit in respect of that breach.

388. Although there is no single formula which can be applied to all cases to determine whether a breach of a continuing one[493], case law suggests that once-and-for all breaches include assigning and underletting[494] as well as making alterations to the demised

[491] Paragraph 34.

[492] Paragraph 37.

[493] See *Downie v Turner* [1951] 2 KB 112

[494] See *Scala House Ltd v Forbes* [1974] 1 QB 575 at 585C, 587E, 588E and 591D.

premises. In each case, the act which constitutes the breach occurs at a single point in time.

389. In contrast, a breach of a user covenant is likely to be a continuing breach. Each day, continuing the use of the premises which is in breach of covenant is a fresh breach.

Method of forfeiture

390. A commercial lease may be forfeited in one of two ways: (1) by the landlord physically re-entering and securing the premises and (2) by the issuing of proceedings for possession. Where part of the premises is let as a dwelling, forfeiture by peaceable re-entry is prohibited *"while any person is lawfully residing in the premises or part of them"*.[495]

Restrictions on forfeiture

391. Covenants to *"keep or put premises in repair during the currency of a lease, or to leave or put premises in repair at the termination of a lease"* are subject to s18(2) of the Landlord and Tenant Act 1927 which provides that a right of forfeiture for breach of such a covenant shall not be enforceable unless the lessor:

a) Proves that a s146 notice was both served on and known to:

i. The lessee; or

ii. An underlessee holding an underlease; or

iii. The person who last paid rent due under the lease; and

[495] See s2 of the Protection from Eviction Act 1977. The Court of Appeal held in *Pirabakaran v Patel* [2006] EWCA Civ 685 held that the references in s2 to premises *"let as a dwelling"* includes premises let partly as a dwelling, meaning that the restriction catches premises let for mixed residential and business purposes.

b) That a *"time reasonably sufficient to enable the repairs to be executed had elapsed since the time when the fact of the service of the notice came to the knowledge of any such person"*.

392. The Leasehold Repairs Act 1938 imposes a number of additional requirements before a lease can be forfeited for breach of a repairing covenant. The 1938 Act only applies where, at the date of service of the s146 notice, *"three or more years of the term of the lease remain unexpired"*[496]. Where the 1938 Act applies, the scheme is as follows:

a) The landlord must serve on the tenant a s.146 notice containing the information prescribed by the Act;

b) The tenant has the right within 28 days of the service of the landlord's notice to serve on the landlord counter-notice claiming the benefit of the Act;

c) If the tenant fails to serve counter-notice within the 28 day period, the Act ceases to apply in relation to the breaches specified in the notice, and the landlord is free to forfeit or claim for damages provided that it would otherwise have the right to do so;

d) If the tenant serves counter-notice within the 28-day period, the landlord cannot either forfeit or begin an action for damages without the leave of the court;

e) The court will only grant leave if (i) the landlord proves one or more of the grounds in s1(5) of the Act, and (ii) the court is satisfied in the exercise of its discretion that leave ought to be granted. The court has power to grant leave subject to conditions;

f) The landlord is not entitled to the benefit of s146(3) of the Law of Property Act 1925 in relation to his solicitor's and

[496] Section s1(1).

surveyor's costs unless he applies for leave and the court so directs.

393. Restrictions are also made on the ability to forfeit the leases of residential property.[497]

Relief from forfeiture

394. A tenant can apply to the court to obtain relief from forfeiture. Whether to grant relief from forfeiture, and on what conditions, is a matter for the discretion of the court but this will ordinarily include remedying the breaches of covenant and paying the landlord's costs on an indemnity basis.[498]

Claims for damages

395. In any damages claim, the landlord will need to prove that the breach of covenant by the tenant has caused the landlord reasonably foreseeable losses.

396. Damages claims are most likely to arise at the expiry of the term as the landlord will find it easier to prove loss to its reversion. During the term, forfeiture and (potentially) injunctive relief are likely to be more appropriate remedies.

397. Section 18(1) of the Landlord and Tenant Act 1927 imposes a statutory cap on damages for breaches of repairing covenants. In cases where the section applies the damages recoverable by the landlord shall not *"exceed the amount (if any) by which the value of the reversion (whether immediate or not) in the premises is diminished owing to the breach of such covenant"*. Further, no damages are

---

[497] See sections 166 to 170 of the Commonhold and Leasehold Reform Act 2002, and s81 of the Housing Act 1996. The 2002 Act provisions do not apply to "*tenancy to which Part 2 of the Landlord and Tenant Act 1954 (c. 56) (business tenancies) applies*" (s169(4)(a)).

[498] On the requirement to pay indemnity costs – see *Patel v K&J Restaurants Ltd* [2010] EWCA Civ 1211; [2011] L & TR 6.

recoverable where it is shown that the premises, in *"whatever state of repair they might be, would at or shortly after the termination of the tenancy have been or be pulled down, or such structural alterations made therein as would render valueless the repairs covered by the covenant or agreement."*

Claims for injunctive relief

398. As above, claims for injunctive relief are perhaps more likely to arise during the term as the landlord will find it more difficult to prove loss to its reversion, which is necessary for a claim in damages. Cases where a claim for an injunction might be appropriate include where the tenant is threatening to perform an act which the landlord considers will breach an alteration, alienation or user covenant. In such a case, the anticipated breach could be restrained by injunction.

399. Injunctions are a discretionary remedy and will ordinarily not be awarded where damages would be an adequate remedy.

400. More powerful justifications will be needed from a landlord before the court will impose a mandatory order upon a tenant requiring them do specified acts than before a court will impose a negative order prohibiting certain acts. This is because the burden of a mandatory injunction is more severe.

Summary

401. In summary:

a) Where a landlord unreasonably refuses consent under a fully qualified covenant, the tenant is entitled to proceed with the subject matter of its application (i.e. assign, underlet, alter the premises/user) without the need for consent, and to do so will not amount to a breach of the covenant;

b) However, the tenant will not have any claim for damages against the landlord for an unreasonable refusal of consent;

c) Tenants should think carefully before pursuing this option. It can be high risk because, if the landlord subsequently establishes that the refusal of consent was reasonable, then the tenant will be in breach of covenant;

d) An alternative option open to tenants is to commence legal proceedings and claim a declaration that consent has been unreasonably withheld;

e) Where the provisions of the Landlord and Tenant Act 1988 apply and a landlord fails to comply with the statutory duties imposed, a tenant which has suffered loss as a result may bring a damages claim for breach of statutory duty;

f) Where a lease contains a forfeiture clause, the landlord may forfeit the lease in the event of a tenant breach of covenant:

g) For breaches other than the non-payment of rent, prior to forfeiture a s146 notice must first be served and the tenant permitted a reasonable time to remedy the breach;

h) Breaches of covenant are capable of remedy for these purposes if the mischief caused by the breach can be put right. On the current state of the case law:

    i. Breaches of alteration covenants will typically be remediable. The question is whether the alterations can in fact be undone;

    ii. Breaches of user covenants will typically be remediable by ceasing the unauthorised use. However, the case law recognises some exceptions – specially where the nature of the prohibited user is immoral and stigmatises the premises;

    iii. The position for breaches of alienation covenants is somewhat uncertain. On the current state of the case law:

1. A breach of a covenant not to assign is likely irremediable. By the same reasoning, the breach of a covenant against sub-letting is also irremediable;

2. Not all breaches of an alienation covenant are incapable of remedy. The Court of Appeal has held that the sharing of possession or occupation which falls short of creating or transferring a legal interest is capable of remedy;

3. The question of whether charging a lease is irremediable is uncertain;

i) The right to forfeit is an option reserved to the landlord – it is up to the landlord whether to take advantage of it or not. The landlord is put to election – and if the landlord elects not to forfeit, the right to forfeit in respect of the breach is waived;

j) A waiver of the right to forfeit will occur where the landlord does acts which are consistent only with treating the lease as continuing (and so are inconsistent with electing to determine it by forfeiture).

k) If the right to forfeit for a once-and-for breach is waived, the right is lost forever. If the right to forfeit for a continuing breach of covenant is waived, a fresh breach occurs the next day and there is a new right to forfeit in respect of that breach;

l) Case law suggests that once-and-for all breaches include assigning and underletting as well as making alterations to the demised premises. In contrast, a breach of a user covenant is likely to be a continuing breach;

m) A tenant can apply to the court to obtain relief from forfeiture. Whether to grant relief from forfeiture, and on what conditions, is a matter for the discretion of the court but this will ordinarily include remedying the breaches of covenant and paying the landlord's costs on an indemnity basis.

MORE BOOKS BY LAW BRIEF PUBLISHING

A selection of our other titles available now:-

'A Practical Guide to Parental Alienation in Private and Public Law Children Cases' by Sam King QC & Frankie Shama
'Contested Heritage – Removing Art from Land and Historic Buildings' by Richard Harwood QC, Catherine Dobson, David Sawtell
'The Limits of Separate Legal Personality: When Those Running a Company Can Be Held Personally Liable for Losses Caused to Third Parties Outside of the Company' by Dr Mike Wilkinson
'A Practical Guide to Transgender Law' by Robin Moira White & Nicola Newbegin
'Artificial Intelligence – The Practical Legal Issues (2nd Edition)' by John Buyers
'A Practical Guide to Residential Freehold Conveyancing' by Lorraine Richardson
'A Practical Guide to Pensions on Divorce for Lawyers' by Bryan Scant
'A Practical Guide to Challenging Sham Marriage Allegations in Immigration Law' by Priya Solanki
'A Practical Guide to Legal Rights in Scotland' by Sarah-Jane Macdonald
'A Practical Guide to New Build Conveyancing' by Paul Sams & Rebecca East
'A Practical Guide to Defending Barristers in Disciplinary Cases' by Marc Beaumont
'A Practical Guide to Inherited Wealth on Divorce' by Hayley Trim
'A Practical Guide to Practice Direction 12J and Domestic Abuse in Private Law Children Proceedings' by Rebecca Cross & Malvika Jaganmohan
'A Practical Guide to Confiscation and Restraint' by Narita Bahra QC, John Carl Townsend, David Winch
'A Practical Guide to the Law of Forests in Scotland' by Philip Buchan
'A Practical Guide to Health and Medical Cases in Immigration Law' by Rebecca Chapman & Miranda Butler
'A Practical Guide to Bad Character Evidence for Criminal Practitioners by Aparna Rao
'A Practical Guide to Extradition Law post-Brexit' by Myles Grandison et al

'A Practical Guide to Hoarding and Mental Health for Housing Lawyers' by Rachel Coyle
'A Practical Guide to Psychiatric Claims in Personal Injury – 2nd Edition' by Liam Ryan
'Stephens on Contractual Indemnities' by Richard Stephens
'A Practical Guide to the EU Succession Regulation' by Richard Frimston
'A Practical Guide to Solicitor and Client Costs – 2nd Edition' by Robin Dunne
'Constructive Dismissal – Practice Pointers and Principles' by Benjimin Burgher
'A Practical Guide to Religion and Belief Discrimination Claims in the Workplace' by Kashif Ali
'A Practical Guide to the Law of Medical Treatment Decisions' by Ben Troke
'Fundamental Dishonesty and QOCS in Personal Injury Proceedings: Law and Practice' by Jake Rowley
'A Practical Guide to the Law in Relation to School Exclusions' by Charlotte Hadfield & Alice de Coverley
'A Practical Guide to Divorce for the Silver Separators' by Karin Walker
'The Right to be Forgotten – The Law and Practical Issues' by Melissa Stock
'A Practical Guide to Planning Law and Rights of Way in National Parks, the Broads and AONBs' by James Maurici QC, James Neill et al
'A Practical Guide to Election Law' by Tom Tabori
'A Practical Guide to the Law in Relation to Surrogacy' by Andrew Powell
'A Practical Guide to Claims Arising from Fatal Accidents – 2nd Edition' by James Patience
'A Practical Guide to the Ownership of Employee Inventions – From Entitlement to Compensation' by James Tumbridge & Ashley Roughton
'A Practical Guide to Asbestos Claims' by Jonathan Owen & Gareth McAloon
'A Practical Guide to Stamp Duty Land Tax in England and Northern Ireland' by Suzanne O'Hara
'A Practical Guide to the Law of Farming Partnerships' by Philip Whitcomb
'Covid-19, Homeworking and the Law – The Essential Guide to Employment and GDPR Issues' by Forbes Solicitors
'Covid-19 and Criminal Law – The Essential Guide' by Ramya Nagesh
'Covid-19 and Family Law in England and Wales – The Essential Guide' by Safda Mahmood

'A Practical Guide to the Law of Unlawful Eviction and Harassment – 2nd Edition' by Stephanie Lovegrove
'Covid-19, Brexit and the Law of Commercial Leases – The Essential Guide' by Mark Shelton
'A Practical Guide to Costs in Personal Injury Claims – 2nd Edition' by Matthew Hoe
'A Practical Guide to the General Data Protection Regulation (GDPR) – 2nd Edition' by Keith Markham
'Ellis on Credit Hire – Sixth Edition' by Aidan Ellis & Tim Kevan
'A Practical Guide to Working with Litigants in Person and McKenzie Friends in Family Cases' by Stuart Barlow
'Protecting Unregistered Brands: A Practical Guide to the Law of Passing Off' by Lorna Brazell
'A Practical Guide to Secondary Liability and Joint Enterprise Post-Jogee' by Joanne Cecil & James Mehigan
'A Practical Guide to the Pre-Action RTA Claims Protocol for Personal Injury Lawyers' by Antonia Ford
'A Practical Guide to Neighbour Disputes and the Law' by Alexander Walsh
'A Practical Guide to Forfeiture of Leases' by Mark Shelton
'A Practical Guide to Coercive Control for Legal Practitioners and Victims' by Rachel Horman
'A Practical Guide to Rights Over Airspace and Subsoil' by Daniel Gatty
'Tackling Disclosure in the Criminal Courts – A Practitioner's Guide' by Narita Bahra QC & Don Ramble
'A Practical Guide to the Law of Driverless Cars – Second Edition' by Alex Glassbrook, Emma Northey & Scarlett Milligan
'A Practical Guide to TOLATA Claims' by Greg Williams
'A Practical Guide to Elderly Law – 2nd Edition' by Justin Patten
'A Practical Guide to Responding to Housing Disrepair and Unfitness Claims' by Iain Wightwick
'A Practical Guide to the Construction and Rectification of Wills and Trust Instruments' by Edward Hewitt
'A Practical Guide to the Law of Bullying and Harassment in the Workplace' by Philip Hyland
'How to Be a Freelance Solicitor: A Practical Guide to the SRA-Regulated Freelance Solicitor Model' by Paul Bennett

'A Practical Guide to Prison Injury Claims' by Malcolm Johnson
'A Practical Guide to the Small Claims Track - 2nd Edition' by Dominic Bright
'A Practical Guide to Advising Clients at the Police Station' by Colin Stephen McKeown-Beaumont
'A Practical Guide to Antisocial Behaviour Injunctions' by Iain Wightwick
'Practical Mediation: A Guide for Mediators, Advocates, Advisers, Lawyers, and Students in Civil, Commercial, Business, Property, Workplace, and Employment Cases' by Jonathan Dingle with John Sephton
'The Mini-Pupillage Workbook' by David Boyle
'A Practical Guide to Crofting Law' by Brian Inkster
'A Practical Guide to Spousal Maintenance' by Liz Cowell
'A Practical Guide to the Law of Domain Names and Cybersquatting' by Andrew Clemson
'A Practical Guide to the Law of Gender Pay Gap Reporting' by Harini Iyengar
'A Practical Guide to the Rights of Grandparents in Children Proceedings' by Stuart Barlow
'NHS Whistleblowing and the Law' by Joseph England
'Employment Law and the Gig Economy' by Nigel Mackay & Annie Powell
'A Practical Guide to Noise Induced Hearing Loss (NIHL) Claims' by Andrew Mckie, Ian Skeate, Gareth McAloon
'An Introduction to Beauty Negligence Claims – A Practical Guide for the Personal Injury Practitioner' by Greg Almond
'Intercompany Agreements for Transfer Pricing Compliance' by Paul Sutton
'Zen and the Art of Mediation' by Martin Plowman
'A Practical Guide to the SRA Principles, Individual and Law Firm Codes of Conduct 2019 – What Every Law Firm Needs to Know' by Paul Bennett
'A Practical Guide to Adoption for Family Lawyers' by Graham Pegg
'A Practical Guide to Industrial Disease Claims' by Andrew Mckie & Ian Skeate
'A Practical Guide to Redundancy' by Philip Hyland
'A Practical Guide to Vicarious Liability' by Mariel Irvine
'A Practical Guide to Applications for Landlord's Consent and Variation of Leases' by Mark Shelton
'A Practical Guide to Relief from Sanctions Post-Mitchell and Denton' by Peter Causton

‘A Practical Guide to Equity Release for Advisors’ by Paul Sams
‘A Practical Guide to Financial Services Claims’ by Chris Hegarty
‘The Law of Houses in Multiple Occupation: A Practical Guide to HMO Proceedings’ by Julian Hunt
‘Occupiers, Highways and Defective Premises Claims: A Practical Guide Post-Jackson – 2nd Edition’ by Andrew Mckie
‘A Practical Guide to Financial Ombudsman Service Claims’ by Adam Temple & Robert Scrivenor
'A Practical Guide to Advising Schools on Employment Law' by Jonathan Holden
‘A Practical Guide to Running Housing Disrepair and Cavity Wall Claims: 2nd Edition’ by Andrew Mckie & Ian Skeate
‘A Practical Guide to Holiday Sickness Claims – 2nd Edition’ by Andrew Mckie & Ian Skeate
‘Arguments and Tactics for Personal Injury and Clinical Negligence Claims’ by Dorian Williams
‘A Practical Guide to Drone Law’ by Rufus Ballaster, Andrew Firman, Eleanor Clot
‘A Practical Guide to Compliance for Personal Injury Firms Working With Claims Management Companies’ by Paul Bennett
‘RTA Allegations of Fraud in a Post-Jackson Era: The Handbook – 2nd Edition’ by Andrew Mckie
‘RTA Personal Injury Claims: A Practical Guide Post-Jackson’ by Andrew Mckie
‘On Experts: CPR35 for Lawyers and Experts’ by David Boyle
‘An Introduction to Personal Injury Law’ by David Boyle

These books and more are available to order online direct from the publisher at www.lawbriefpublishing.com, where you can also read free sample chapters. For any queries, contact us on 0844 587 2383 or mail@lawbriefpublishing.com.

Our books are also usually in stock at www.amazon.co.uk with free next day delivery for Prime members, and at good legal bookshops such as Wildy & Sons.

We are regularly launching new books in our series of practical day-to-day practitioners' guides. Visit our website and join our free newsletter to be kept informed and to receive special offers, free chapters, etc.

You can also follow us on Twitter at www.twitter.com/lawbriefpub.

www.ingramcontent.com/pod-product-compliance
Lightning Source LLC
LaVergne TN
LVHW052325200926
848481LV00002B/677

* 9 7 8 1 9 1 4 6 0 8 7 7 3 *